Z-Wave Essentials

4th Edition

Prof. Dr.-Ing. Christian Paetz

May 2018

For God so loved the world that he gave his one and only Son, that whoever believes in him shall not perish but have eternal life.

John 3,16 (NIV)

© 2018 Prof. Dr.- Ing. Christian Paetz, 08064 Zwickau

4. Edition 2018, 3. Edition 2017, 2. Edition 2015, 1. Edition 2013,

ISBN: 978-1718708228

Contents

1 Introduction   **10**

1.1 What is a Smart Home? 11

1.2 Smart Home Definitions 17

1.3 General Layer Model of wireless communication network 18

1.4 Requirements of a wireless system for home control 19

1.5 Alternatives for wireless home control networks . . 22

    1.5.1 Analogue Control using 27 MHz or 433 MHz frequency band 22

    1.5.2 Proprietary digital protocols from different vendors 22

    1.5.3 Wi-Fi or WLAN 23

    1.5.4 IEEE 802.15.4 based communication networks 25

    1.5.5 ZigBee 25

    1.5.6 Thread 27

    1.5.7 EnOcean 28

    1.5.8 DECT ULE 29

    1.5.9 Z-Wave 30

1.6 Z-Wave in a nutshell 32

    1.6.1 How it all started 32

    1.6.2 The business model 34

    1.6.3   Z-Wave becomes an open standard 35

    1.6.4   Z-Wave Plus 37

    1.6.5   How to recognize Z-Wave 39

2   Radio Layer   40

  2.1   Wireless Basics 40

  2.2   Frequencies used by Z-Wave 42

    2.2.1   SRD 860 44

    2.2.2   ISM 915 46

    2.2.3   How Z-Wave with different frequencies . . . 47

  2.3   Wireless Range Estimations 49

    2.3.1   Background Noise 52

    2.3.2   Antenna Design and Antenna Loss 54

    2.3.3   Attenuation 56

    2.3.4   Wireless Shadows 60

    2.3.5   Reflections and Interference 60

    2.3.6   Fade Margin 61

    2.3.7   Summary 64

  2.4   Electro Magnetic Energy (EME) and Health 64

3   Z-Wave Networking   67

  3.1   Data Communication with G.9959 67

    3.1.1   The PHY function 67

    3.1.2   Wireless Frame (MAC-Frame) 71

    3.1.3   Home-ID and Node-ID 72

    3.1.4   Network Transport Function 79

    3.1.5   Data Reliability and Error Correction . . . 82

    3.1.6   Acknowledged Communication 84

  3.2   Routing 86

    3.2.1   Routing Basics 86

    3.2.2   The Routing Algorithm 89

  3.3   Device and Network Types 95

    3.3.1   Role in Network: Controller and Slaves . . 95

3.3.2   Different ways to power devices 96

3.3.3   Summary 106

3.4   Manual Update of the network 109

3.4.1   Exclusion - Removal of functioning devices   109

3.4.2   Removal of defective devices - Failed Node List 110

3.4.3   Network Reorganization 113

3.5   Automated Updating of the network 113

3.5.1   Static Update Controller 115

3.5.2   Explorer Frame 118

3.5.3   Explorer frames versus SUC/SIS in one network 122

3.6   Network configurations 125

3.6.1   Z-Wave Network with one portable controller 125

3.6.2   Z-Wave Network with one static controller . 126

3.6.3   Portable and static controller in one network 127

3.6.4   Network with SUC/SIS controller 128

3.6.5   Comparison of different network configurations 128

4   Z-Wave Application Layer   131

4.1   Devices and Commands 131

4.1.1   Types of Z-Wave Devices 131

4.1.2   Command Classes 134

4.1.3   Command Class `Basic` 138

4.1.4   Device Classes 138

4.2   Managing Devices 145

4.2.1   Node Information Frame 145

4.2.2   Interview 147

4.2.3   Configuration 148

4.2.4   Battery Management 151

4.2.5   Maximization of battery lifetime 152

4.2.6   Multichannel Devices 158

4.2.7   Associations 160
4.3   Scenes 166
    4.3.1   Examples 166
    4.3.2   Scene Snapshot 169
    4.3.3   Definition of scenes in central controllers . . 170
    4.3.4   Activation of scenes by timers 172
    4.3.5   Activation of scenes by wireless devices . . 172
    4.3.6   Activation of scenes by Boolean logic 176
    4.3.7   Complex Scenes with Scripting 179
    4.3.8   Comparison of association groups and Scenes 180
4.4   User Interfaces 181
    4.4.1   Wall controllers and remote controls 181
    4.4.2   Installer tools 182
    4.4.3   Web-Interfaces for Users 182
4.5   Wireless Security in Smart Homes 184
    4.5.1   General information about security and typ-
            ical attacks 185
    4.5.2   Encryption 185
    4.5.3   *Replay*-Attacks 186
    4.5.4   *Denial-of-Service-Attack* 189
    4.5.5   Further aspects of wireless security 189
    4.5.6   The conventional security concept of Z-Wave 190
    4.5.7   The security architecture S2 194

5 Z-Wave in action - Tips and Tricks   205
5.1   Building the network - general workflow 205
    5.1.1   Defining the desired functions 205
    5.1.2   Picking the right devices 207
    5.1.3   Z-Wave Wall Switches versus Wall Inserts . 209
    5.1.4   Including everything into a single network . 213
    5.1.5   Way to include devices 214
    5.1.6   Smart Start 218

5.1.7 Inclusion of Controllers 220

5.1.8 Inclusion of battery-operated devices 224

5.1.9 Interview Process 225

5.1.10 Configuration 227

5.1.11 Association and Scenes 228

5.2 Housekeeping - How to get a stable network? . . . 228

5.2.1 Radio Layer 229

5.2.2 Z-Wave Networking and Routing 229

5.3 Trouble Shooting with CIT Tool or Z-Way Expert UI 233

5.3.1 Radio Layer 235

5.3.2 Network Layer - Devices 237

5.3.3 Network Layer - Weak or Wrong Routes . . 243

5.3.4 Application Layer Settings 247

5.3.5 Summary 249

5.4 Known Problems 249

5.4.1 Mismatch of Language 252

5.4.2 Mismatch of functions 252

5.4.3 No forward compatibility 252

5.4.4 Multi Channels versus Multi Instances . . . 254

5.4.5 Sins from the past 255

5.4.6 IP-Gateways 255

5.4.7 Weak Check Sum 256

5.4.8 Turnkey-Solutions 256

6 Special topics around Z-Wave 257

6.1 Legal situation 257

6.1.1 Important Patents of Z-Wave 259

6.1.2 Important Patents challenging Z-Wave . . . 260

6.2 SDKs 263

6.3 How to develop Z-Wave devices 265

6.3.1 Hardware 265

6.3.2   Firmware 267
6.3.3   ZUNO 269
6.3.4   Z-Way Middleware 273
6.3.5   Z-Wave Certification 275
6.4   General information about dimmers 275
6.4.1   Leading-edge phase control 276
6.4.2   Leading Edge Phase Control for inductive
        loads 277
6.4.3   Trailing Edge Phase Control Dimmer . . . 278
6.4.4   Universal Dimmers 280
6.4.5   Fluorescent Lamps 280
6.4.6   LED Lamps 280
6.4.7   Dimmer Summary 281

A Useful Online Resources   282

B Z-Wave Device Types   284

C Z-Wave Command Classes Reference   288

D Frequencies by Country   293

What is new in Spring 2018? Compared to the second version of this book, issued in 2015, the following parts were added or substantially updated:

- (c4) Section on DSK
- (c4) Better explanation of S2 authentication
- (c5) Poltorak Chart
- (c5) Smart Start
- (c6) SDK 6.8x
- Layout Improvement resulting is less pages for more content
- (c1,c3) Series 700
- Z-Wave is now part of Silicon Labs

What is new in Spring 2017? Compared to the second version of this book, issued in 2015, the following parts were added or substantially updated:

- (c1) Update on "other wireless protocols"
- (c1) Z-Wave is now public domain
- (c1) New Section on Z-Wave history, business model, logo history, and Z-Wave Plus
- (c2) Chapter 2 is rewritten from scratch, now focusing on wireless range estimation
- (c3) Explorer Frame process is explained in detail
- (c3) Z-Wave Plus network roles as part of the network section
- (c3) Energy-Harvesting
- (c3) Z-Wave channel concept introduced
- (c3) CRC16 in Z-Wave channel 3
- (c4) Z-Wave+ device types as part of the device class section
- (c4) Multi-channel devices
- (c4) Lifeline
- (c4) Central scene
- (c4) Decentral nature of associations
- (c4) New Security Architecture S2

- (c5) Practical considerations on Interview process.
- (c5) Trouble Shooting of Z-Wave networks using CIT or Z-Way-Expert-UI
- (c5) Problems with turnkey solution of certain manufacturers
- (c6) Development of Z-Wave devices
- Updates on ICs, SDKs, etc.
- Clarification on network architecture on PHY, MAC and Transport layer
- More than 80 % of the images are updated or replaced

What is new in 2015?   Compared to the first version of this book, issued in 2013, the following parts were added or substantially updated:

- Security in Z-Wave
- Update to Series 500 chips
- Update to FLIRS
- Update to Auto inclusion as the new default way to include
- Z-Wave Plus
- Comparison between Wall Inserts and Wall Switches

Chapter 1

Introduction

Z-Wave is an international standard of wireless communications for home automation. It interconnects different devices such as lighting, heating, climate control, media and entertainment, safety equipment, and security systems. The interconnection of multiple systems creates a smart home where devices from different vendors work together, thereby enhancing safety, security, convenience, and the quality of life of the people living in that environment. More importantly, a smart home helps to save energy and to protect human life and the environment.

The key to smart home automation is the interconnection of various devices and the ability to control all of them through a single user interface, which may be a web browser, a wall touch panel, a dedicated remote control, or a mobile phone.

The interconnection of devices in a residential home requires common communication media. There are three different approaches to this:

- Wired solutions require dedicated cables to be installed during construction or major house renovation. Wired solutions such as BACNet (a protocol that runs on different media types), and certain versions of LON or KNX, namely Instabus in Europe, are generally expensive and therefore used in commercial installations and very high-end residential homes.

- Powerline communication uses 110 V or 230 V mains power installation as communication media. Certain standards such as HomeplugAV are more common, but they are mainly used as a replacement for Ethernet technology applied for media distributions such as TV, video, and audio.
- Wireless solutions show the biggest growth in the market since they are both reliable and affordable and can be applied in homes without major refurbishments. Additionally, certain technologies such as intelligent door locks or sensors can hardly be installed with wires because they are used on moving devices such as doors.

Therefore, wireless technologies can be considered the future basis for interconnecting devices in a smart home.

1.1 What is a Smart Home?

"Smart home" is a term often used along with the more descriptive term "home automation." Wikipedia defines home automation as:

> **"Home automation is the residential extension of 'building automation.' It is automation of the home, housework or household activity. Home automation may include centralized control of lighting, HVAC (heating, ventilation and air conditioning), appliances, and other systems, to provide improved convenience, comfort, energy efficiency and security. Home automation for the elderly and disabled can provide increased quality of life for persons who might otherwise require caregivers or institutional care. A home automation system inte-**

grates electrical devices in a house with each other. The techniques employed in home automation include those in building automation as well as the control of domestic activities, such as home entertainment systems, houseplant and yard watering, pet feeding, changing the ambiance "scenes" for different events (such as dinners or parties), and the use of domestic robots. Devices may be connected through a computer network to allow control by a personal computer, and may allow remote access from the Internet. Through the integration of information technologies with the home environment, systems and appliances are able to communicate in an integrated manner, which results in convenience, energy efficiency, and safety benefits." [SmartHome2017]

The definition is accurate but not very insightful. Let's start with the obvious: In the good old time, the controlling part and the controlled part of a function in the home were located in the same device. A candle was lit right at the candle and the light came right from the candle. A door knocker was operated right at the device and generated noise right at the same device.

The advent of electricity in the last 100 years has partly changed this reality. The electronic door bell is operated at the door by pressing a button and the more or less ugly sound of the bell comes from a 'bell' connected with the door button by an electrical circuit. The electrical light is typically controlled by a wall switch that is no longer located right next to the light bulb but in a convenient location next to the door where the resident can easily access it when entering the room. Again, the wall switch is connected to light bulbs via an electrical circuit.

Other examples are the control of the window blinds, the wall thermostats controlling the heat in the room, or a simple remote

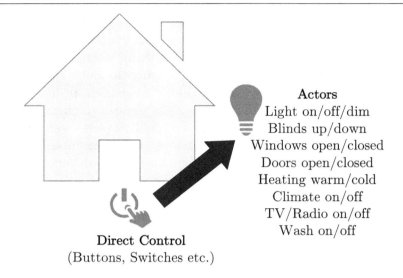

Actors
Light on/off/dim
Blinds up/down
Windows open/closed
Doors open/closed
Heating warm/cold
Climate on/off
TV/Radio on/off
Wash on/off

Direct Control
(Buttons, Switches etc.)

Figure 1.1: Traditional home of the late 1990s

control turning on and off devices that are inconvenient to access directly. The home is mixed with various devices that are still controlled and operated right from the devices. Examples of such devices include dishwasher, washing machine, dryer, or electric stove. TVs moved out of this category about 40 years ago when the infrared remote control became the standard device to control them.

Image 1.1 shows the situation in a traditional home of the early 21st century, reflecting the different ways to control devices in the home. The smart home or home automation changes this situation in multiple ways.

To begin with, the direct relationship between device and control of the device is relaxed. The light switch may no longer only control a light but as well other functions of the room. A remote control is no longer dedicated to one single device but to multiple entertainment devices and home functions such as light or climate

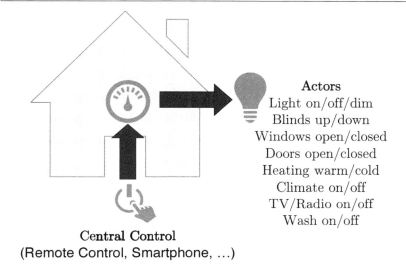

Figure 1.2: First step into Smart Home

control.

Image 1.2 demonstrates this first step into the smart home. This first step offers a first simplification of usage and control to the resident. It unifies the operations concept and allows using a more convenient single point of control. Good examples of such single points of control are mobile phones, which have largely become the central point of control to various functions and services in people's lives.

The second step into a smart home is the use of sensors that give further information about the status of the home and actions to be undertaken to improve the convenience and security of the resident. By no means this is a new concept. Wall thermostats contain a temperature sensor that is used to control the heating in the room and the smoke detector is also a sensor as such. The concept of a smart home brings the idea of a sensor controlling the room to a new level. Motion detectors control the light if

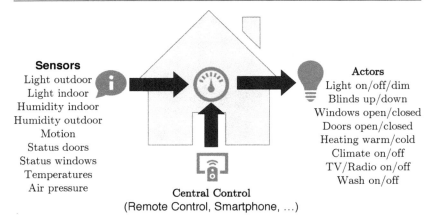

Sensors
Light outdoor
Light indoor
Humidity indoor
Humidity outdoor
Motion
Status doors
Status windows
Temperatures
Air pressure

Central Control
(Remote Control, Smartphone, …)

Actors
Light on/off/dim
Blinds up/down
Windows open/closed
Doors open/closed
Heating warm/cold
Climate on/off
TV/Radio on/off
Wash on/off

Figure 1.3: Second step into Smart Home

people are in a room or turn down or even off the heating when
people have left the room. Air quality sensors control windows
and ventilation to guarantee enough oxygen in the room when
occupied. This second step is represented by Image 1.3.

Last but not least, the core function of a smart home is automation. An intelligent entity aggregates the different information
given either by sensors or by the resident's interactions—e.g. operating a button—to create intelligent control of the different
functions of the home. This entity is able to make decisions on
functions automatically, and partly without any interaction by
the user.

A good example is the control of a roof window. In wintertime,
the windows shall be closed with shutters during the night to
preserve as much energy as possible. During the day, the window
blinds may go up, and at noon, if the outside temperature is
sensed to be high enough, the windows open automatically to
bring fresh air into the room. A rain and a wind sensor provide
information to keep the window closed during heavy wind or

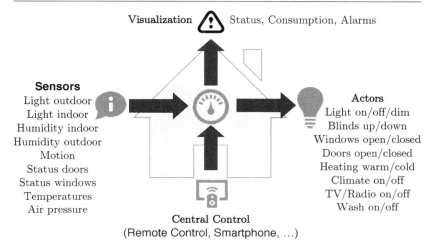

Figure 1.4: Final step into Smart Home

rain. In summertime, the automation may be different. Now the window shall be closed during daytime with blinds down to prevent overheating and it shall open up at night to get fresh air into the room. Of course, rain and wind protection are provided as well. If the automation control is aware that the resident is not in the building, the windows may be closed 24 hours for security reasons.

Besides the control of the home, the interconnected system of sensors and acting devices—also referred to as actuators—can provide information about certain measurement values for determining the status of the home and the resident. This may not only help to further optimize the functions of the home but also inform the user about the safety and security and help to conserve energy when possible.

Image 1.4 shows this final step into a smart home. Home owners want to be informed about what is going on and contemporary 'user interfaces' such as wall panels or mobile phones will provide information about the status of the home and also alert in case of events.

The characteristics of a smart home can be defined as

> **"Different unified user interfaces control different actions in the home using the users interaction, sensor data and intelligent decisions made by the control itself. The same time the smart home provides useful information for the resident to help to make smarter decisions such as conserving energy."**

1.2 Smart Home Definitions

There are some common characteristics and basic language used in every smart home environment.

- **Sensor:** A sensor is a device that generates information and delivers it to other devices in the network using a communication network. Examples of such sensors are the temperature sensors in the room thermostat, motion detectors, door sensors, or smoke detectors.
- **Controllers:** Controllers are devices that control other devices using the communication network between them. They typically provide a user interface. Examples of controllers are remote controls, keypads, and wall switches.
- **Actors:** Actors—also referred to as actuators—are devices that perform an action. They switch, dim, turn on or off, wind up, shut down, etc. Examples of actors are window motors, light switches, light dimmers, electronic door locks.
- **Control Network:** The network is the communication medium that interconnects actors, controllers, and sensors.
- **Gateways:** Gateways interconnect the home communication network to other communication networks such as Transmission Control Protocol/Internet Protocol (TCP/IP)-

based Internet or the cell phone network.

The intelligence of the home control network may reside in one single device. This is typically the gateway because it needs higher computing power. However, the function may also be distributed among various devices.

Certain devices may also mix different functions in one single hardware device. Multiple sensors - e.g. temperature or humidity are very common. Another example of such a hybrid device is a room thermostat, which typically combines a temperature sensor with a user interface to set the desired temperature in the room.

1.3 General Layer Model of wireless communication network

Communication systems are complex and consist of a huge number of functions. In order to structure all these functions, communication engineers cluster them into a layer stack or a protocol stack. The idea of the layer stack is that one layer uses the services of the underlying layer and provides a function to the layer above. Their functions are well defined so it is at least theoretically possible to replace one implementation of a layer by a different implementation without changing the rest of the stack. Each layer has its defined functions to be performed and these functions define the services one layer offers to the upper layer. For communication networks in a smart home, a four-layer structure is commonly used:

1. **Radio Layer:** This layer defines the way a signal is exchanged between a transmitter and a receiver. This includes issues like frequency, encoding, hardware access, etc. The radio layer transports different bits and bytes from one device to another device. **"Makes sure a bit travels from one node to another node."**

2. **Network Layer:** This layer makes sure that data are

transmitted securely and reliably from the source to the destination. In a wireless radio network, this may require using certain devices as wireless repeaters. The functions of the network layer include the organization of the network (who is in, who is out), addressing, routing, encryption, data retransmission, and data. **'Makes sure the right bit stream travels from the sender to the receiver.'**

3. **Application Layer:** The application layer defines the meaning of the data transmitted by the network layer and subsequently the radio layer. The network layer only knows bytes. The application layer defines the meaning of the bytes and explains how they form a command. The application layer defines the format of metering and measuring the values and different commands used to perform certain actions. **'Makes sure the receiver understands the intention of the sender and acts accordingly.'**

4. **User interface:** The user interface layer acts as an interface to the user itself. It defines how certain functions of the network and certain status information are presented on different user interfaces such as a cell phone, tablet screen, or even a wall switch. The user interface defines features like meanings of icons, LED blinking sequences, and the number and speed of needed button presses. **'Makes sure the user understands the situation in the system.'**

This four-layer structure is shown in Figure 1.5. This book will organize the description of the Z-Wave wireless communication world using this layer model.

1.4 Requirements of a wireless system for home control

The communication network of a smart home needs to meet a set of requirements. Since wireless technologies are clearly the winning choice compared to wire-based technology, the following

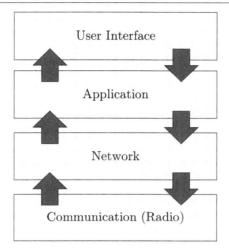

Figure 1.5: Generic four layers of a wireless communication network

comparison will focus on wireless technologies.

The requirements are:

1. **Reliability of the communication:** It is essential for important functions such as door locks, alarm, and heating to be reliable. In order to ensure this reliability, it is important that all messages reach their destination and are confirmed by the receiving device back to the transmitter. This two-way communication, where every message sent is confirmed or acknowledged back to the transmitter, is what defines a reliable communication. Not all wireless network technologies meet this requirement.

2. **Security of communication:** It must be guaranteed that an unauthorized third party cannot purposely or even accidentally intercept or interfere with the communication system. Typically, encoding or encryption technologies and handshake mechanisms ensure this.

3. **Low-power radio emission:** For health and safety, as well as interference with other wireless devices such as phones, radios, and TVs, it is essential that the wireless technology for home automation is as low-powered as possible. This is also helpful in achieving extended battery life for battery-powered devices.

4. **Simple usage:** Home automation will make the life of the user easier and not more complicated.

5. **Adequate price:** Price is an obvious point to ensure broad acceptance of the technology.

6. **Protection of investment:** Home automation solutions are typically installed during the construction or renovation of buildings and need to comply with the typical product life cycles of home installation equipment. It is important to ensure that users are able to replace devices or extend their systems even after years without facing any compatibility issue.

7. **Interoperability:** Home automation functions such as heating, lighting, and window control are implemented with products from different vendors each with expertise in their respective areas. It is not acceptable to stick with one vendor and buy, for example, heating technology from a vendor with core competence in lighting, just to enable interoperability of all system devices. Each installed wireless technology has to be used without consideration of several manufacturers.

   Cross-vendor interoperability is ensured by strong technology standards and product certification programs. Good examples of interoperability are Wi-Fi, Bluetooth, and Z-Wave.

1.5 Alternatives for wireless home control networks

There are various wireless communication technologies for smart homes that comply more or less with the requirements just outlined.

1.5.1 Analogue Control using 27 MHz or 433 MHz frequency band

Analogue wireless systems are typically available from unnamed vendors and are remarkably cheap. Their strong focus on entry-level performance and a low price typically results in low manufacturing quality and very poor security. Because the frequency used is often shared with baby monitor radios or CB transceivers, interference is common and the equipment behaves unpredictably. Because of these limitations, analogue wireless systems are not widely used for more serious installations in homes. They are increasingly being replaced by digital systems that are more reliable and have higher levels of performance and flexibility.

1. **Reliability of communication:** no
2. **Security of communication:** no
3. **Low radio emission:** yes
4. **Simple usage:** yes
5. **Low price:** yes
6. **Protection of investment:** no
7. **Interoperability:** no

1.5.2 Proprietary digital protocols from different vendors

Multiple manufacturers have developed their own proprietary digital solutions for wireless control and some of them offer a variety of products. Some of these protocols have implemented a two-way reliable communication with full acknowledgement of transmission.

By far, the biggest disadvantage of these solutions is that the communication technology used is proprietary or private to one or a very small number of vendors. This does not pose a problem for a simple solution but often prevents the implementation of a complete automation or control solution. Not only are the types of products limited, but, due to the small number of vendors, there is the risk of long-term availability of products. It is not uncommon to see vendors change protocols and make some previous products obsolete. Nevertheless, proprietary technologies play their role in the market mainly because of substantial marketing efforts from the companies owning these technologies and their one-stop simplicity in purchasing.

1. **Reliability of communication:** partly
2. **Security of communication:** partly
3. **Low radio emission:** yes
4. **Simple usage:** yes
5. **Low price:** yes
6. **Protection of investment:** no
7. **Interoperability:** no

1.5.3   Wi-Fi or WLAN

Wireless LAN (Wi-Fi), also referred to as Wi-Fi, is most likely the technology with the highest market penetration. Virtually all notebooks, netbooks, tablet PCs, and almost all smartphones have Wi-Fi interface built in. This raises the obvious question why smart homes are not utilizing Wi-Fi as the standard communication network. There are three reasons for this:

(1) Wi-Fi is designed for transmitting a large amount of data and hence uses a lot of energy for transmission and reception. Speed, high security, and large transmission ratio come at a big price: Wi-Fi takes way too much energy for a home control network

that is at least partly built on battery-powered devices or even devices using energy harvesting. Therefore, Wi-Fi can be used in parts of the smart home where devices are powered by mains power. However, it cannot cover the whole range of applications. The interconnection between smart home devices and cell phones or tablets is typically achieved using Wi-Fi to a gateway device. Then some other lower speed and lower power technology is used from the gateway to the end devices, sensors, and actuators. There have been various attempts at decreasing the power consumption of Wi-Fi, but none of them comes nearly to a level where battery-operated devices can be used at a reasonable battery life.

(2) Wi-Fi uses frequencies around 2.4 GHz and 5 GHz, which are heavily congested. At the moment, this is not yet a big problem in typical residential homes, but more and more high-energy Wi-Fi transmitters are getting deployed usually for digital media streaming. Users of Netflix, WirelessHD, and other heavy-bandwidth services create a big future risk for any technology with lower bandwidth and lower transmitting power that shares the same spectrum. Exhibitors at trade shows are aware that a certain number of active Wi-Fi devices in a room could shut down all Wi-Fi communication.

(3) Wi-Fi only specifies the radio layer and the network layer. There is no generally accepted application layer specification for smart homes based on Wi-Fi. This means that different devices using Wi-Fi can work in one single network but cannot interoperate. The Internet Engineering Task Force (IETF) as a standardization body of the Internet application layers is working on this issue, but so far there is no widely accepted standard. The only currently available link between Internet/Wi-Fi technology and smart homes is the so-called 6LoWPAN specification [6LoWPAN2017]. 6LoWPAN defines how to map an IP V6 address to the addresses used in the Internet and to wireless technologies typically used in smart homes. The aim is to create the

Internet of things where each device in the home has its own IP address and is reachable from the Internet. The reader may decide whether this is a desirable solution from the security and privacy point of view.

1. **Reliability of communication:** mainly yes
2. **Security of communication:** yes
3. **Low radio emission:** no
4. **Simple usage:** yes
5. **Low price:** yes
6. **Protection of investment:** no proprietary application layer
7. **Interoperability:** no proprietary application layer

1.5.4   IEEE 802.15.4 based communication networks

The standard IEEE 802.15.4 defines a reliable low-power, low-data rate communication link that is used as the underlying layer for a variety of different home automation communication network technologies. The specification leaves plenty of room for proprietary implementation because it only specifies the radio layer. This limits the specification benefit to the use of common hardware, resulting in lower prices for the ICs.

Consequently, IEEE 802.15.4 radios are by far the most-deployed small band radios. A number of proprietary wireless communication solutions and products are based on this technology. However, since there is no definition of higher communication layers, the standard cannot be referred to as a complete communication network solution.

1.5.5   ZigBee

ZigBee is certainly the most prominent communication protocol using IEEE 802.15.4 as its radio link. Essentially, ZigBee is a specification of a network layer only. Some application layer specifications were added later, but they were never made mandatory.

This leads to a broad variety of ZigBee implementations coexisting in the market. All these versions claim to be ZigBee—and they are even justified in doing so—but none of them is interoperable with others.

To solve the problem, Zigbee introduced certain application profiles and a certification process. However, the situation eventually got worse. Now ZigBee offers a series of official versions of the standard while the vendor-specific applications coexist in the market.

The following list shows all the specifications and standards currently available and labeled as ZigBee (according to Wikipedia Jan 2017).

1. Various Specs
    (a) ZigBee Home Automation 1.2
    (b) ZigBee Smart Energy 1.1b
    (c) ZigBee Telecommunication Services 1.0
    (d) ZigBee Health Care 1.0
    (e) ZigBee RF4CE - Remote Control 1.0
    (f) ZigBee RF4CE - Input Device 1.0
    (g) ZigBee Remote Control 2.0
    (h) ZigBee Light Link 1.0
    (i) ZigBee IP 1.0
    (j) ZigBee Building Automation 1.0
    (k) ZigBee Gateway 1.0
    (l) ZigBee Green Power 1.0 as optional feature of ZigBee 2012
    (m) ZigBee Retail Services
2. Specs in development
    (a) ZigBee Smart Energy 2.0
    (b) ZigBee Smart Energy 1.2/1.3
    (c) ZigBee Light Link 1.1
    (d) ZigBee Home Automation 1.3

It is to be noted that this is only a list of the public specifications. Most of the implementations will further "improve" the specs and make them vendor-proprietary again.

The freedom to do this makes Zigbee a great technology for companies that want to avoid interoperability with other vendors but lock-in their customers to their specific solution. Hence, the largest installation base of Zigbee devices is found in application spaces where one vendor supplies the whole solution and no connection to other devices is needed.

Apart from the interoperability problem, Zigbee is increasingly challenged by its security loopholes and interference problems caused by the use of the congested 2.4 GHz frequency band [Markoffnov2016].

1. **Reliability of communication:** usually yes
2. **Security of communication:** soso
3. **Low radio emission:** yes
4. **Simple usage:** not yet
5. **Low price:** not yet
6. **Protection of investment:** not yet
7. **Interoperability:** yes at radio layer, not yet at application layer due to too many profiles and low vendor adoption of profiles

1.5.6   Thread

Another adopter of the IEEE 802.15.4 radio is the Thread Group. Thread was founded in 2014 by a group of companies around Nest, a Google Alphabet daughter company selling thermostats for smart homes. The involvement of some large companies like Google and Samsung had already given the initiative a lot of press coverage and public attention. However, it was not until 2016 that a first specification of a protocol was made public. Unfortunately, the specification is already split into two not interoperable versions even before initial devices are in the market. Like Zigbee, Thread defines the networking layer of the communication stack and leaves the application layer open to others.

Thread claims to be IP due to its use of 6LoWPAN mapping of the IP V6 addresses used.

1. **Reliability of communication:** yes
2. **Security of communication:** yes
3. **Low radio emission:** yes
4. **Simple usage:** not known
5. **Low price:** yes
6. **Protection of investment:** not yet
7. **Interoperability:** not yet

1.5.7 EnOcean

Founded in 2001, EnOcean GmbH is a spin-off company of the German company Siemens AG. EnOcean actors and sensors work without battery using energy-harvesting techniques, meaning energy generated out of thin air. The claim of battery-free devices using energy from the air has great appeal in our environment-oriented society. This claim, however, comes at a cost: The communication is not as reliable as other technologies such as ZigBee or Z-Wave and the devices are comparably costly. The low power available from energy harvesting such as piezo effect for buttons, solar panels, or peltier elements generating energy from temperature differences also heavily limit the wireless range of EnOcean. The company offers repeaters to overcome this restriction. The low radio range and low communication security caused by the lack of energy make EnOcean only interesting in application where security and range are less important. This is the case for light control, particularly in industrial buildings, where the company has its sweet spot. EnOcean has been attempting to enter the residential market, but the higher price of the components and lack of security have blocked the road so far. Moreover, Enocean is not plug and play and requires special knowledge to be installed and configured.

1. **Reliability of communication:** no
2. **Security of communication:** no

3. **Low radio emission:** yes
4. **Simple usage:** yes
5. **Low price:** no
6. **Protection of investment:** yes
7. **Interoperability:** yes

1.5.8   DECT ULE

Digital Enhanced Cordless Telecommunications (DECT, initially Digital European Cordless Telephony) is an international standard of cordless phones (with base station in the room or in the house) but not of mobile phones).

The market for cordless phones is declining, primarily due to the increasing use of normal mobile phones and Wi-Fi-based devices within private homes. Therefore, the vendors of the technology have looked for a new use of their investment and knowledge. In 2011 the initially power-hungry DECT technology was enhanced by power-reducing functions and the new protocol was called DECT ULE (ULE = ultra-low energy). DECT ULE is now suitable for battery-operated devices.

The big advantage of DECT is the possession of a frequency band around 1800 MHz that is not jammed by higher-power radio products such as Wi-Fi.

The industry alliance DECT ULE seeks to standardize the application functions of DECT, but there is yet no market relevance of this technology. The deployment of other technologies such as ZigBee and Z-Wave has shown that this process takes many years. It may be that DECT ULE is simply too late for the smart home market.

1. **Reliability of communication:** yes
2. **Security of communication:** yes
3. **Low radio emission:** yes
4. **Simple usage:** not known
5. **Low price:** not known

6. **Protection of investment:** likely
7. **Interoperability:** not known yet

1.5.9   Z-Wave

Z-Wave was especially designed as a wireless communication technology for residential homes. No wonder that it has all the ingredients to perfectly service this market. The main advantages of Z-Wave are as follows:

- use of sub-1GHz frequency avoiding the heavily congested 2.4 GHz and 5 GHz bands where Wi-Fi and ZigBee are positioned.
- secure and reliable two-way communication using message acknowledgement and mesh networking (for definition and explanation of mesh network, please refer to 3.2).
- reasonable price point, certainly higher than the low end analog technologies but substantially lower than high-end technologies such as EnOcean, which are dedicated to the professional building market.
- Z-Wave ensures 100 % interoperability as its core value. All devices that implement Z-Wave will work together in one single network and can be controlled from every controller that also uses Z-Wave.

1. **Reliability of communication:** yes
2. **Security of communication:** yes
3. **Low radio emission:** yes
4. **Simple usage:** yes
5. **Low price:** not yet
6. **Protection of investment:** yes
7. **Interoperability:** yes

Table 1.1 summarizes the pros and cons of the different protocols.

Technology	Pro	Con
Analog	inexpensive	Unreliable, not interoperable
Digital	Proprietary	Not interoperable
Wi-Fi	Widely used, available in cell phones, etc, low price	Not interoperable, high energy consumption / no batteries possible
ZigBee	Stable standard, low cost ICs	Not interoperable
Z-Wave	Interoperable, reliable	Cost higher than analog systems, not (yet) available in notebooks, cell phones, ...
Thread	low cost ICs, bit players like Google behind it	few devices,no interoperability
DECT ULE	Interoperable, reliable	few devices, a late comer
EnOcean	No batteries, interoperable	High price, low security

Table 1.1: Summary of Pros and Cons of different radio technologies

Figure 1.6: The first Z-Wave Controller made by Zensys in 2001 keys granted (Source: Z-Wave Alliance)

1.6 Z-Wave in a nutshell

1.6.1 How it all started

Z-Wave was developed by a Danish company named Zensys. Two Danish engineers founded Zensys toward the end of the 1990s in Copenhagen. The initial idea was to develop a wireless home automation and light control system. Figure 1.6 shows the very first controller device made by Zensys.

The company soon realized that there is a much bigger market by focusing on the wireless technology and licensing it to third parties such as by selling a special ASIC and providing all the embedded software needed to implement a smart home system.

Making this reliable and interoperable technology available to manufacturers world wide has resulted in the largest ecosystem of manufacturers with compatible products.

Figure 1.7: Z-Wave Alliance Website (as of 2017)

Zensys's first major customers were from the US, where, thanks to an early powerline carrier home automation protocol called X10, a relevant market and market awareness had already existed for home automation.

Another watershed moment in the Z-Wave development was the foundation of the Z-Wave Alliance in 2005. In this industrial alliance, the manufacturers of Z-Wave-compatible products are gathered. The Z-Wave Alliance enhances the standard and also takes care of central marketing events such as trade shows. Another central responsibility of the Z-Wave Alliance is the maintenance of the interoperability of the devices based on the Z-Wave protocol. This is guaranteed by a certification program that gives a logo on the device guaranteeing the compliance with the Z-Wave standard.

In 2008, the Danish startup Zensys was acquired by the US chipmaker Sigma Designs (NASDAQ: SIGM). This company has since been driving the development of the technology. In 2018 the Texas Chip company Silicon Labs(NASDAQ: SLABS) acquired the Z-Wave business from Sigma Designs.

1.6.2   The business model

The business model of Zensys (Silicon Labs) in terms of Z-Wave has not changed all these years. The company focuses on the design and production of a special application-specific integrated circuit (ASIC) and the lower layers of the communication protocol software. The ASIC is released in so-called "series" with some variations on ICs in terms of pin-out and performance.

The first-generation Z-Wave hardware was sold from 2003 onward, at that time still as a combination of a standard microcontroller (Atmel) and a radio transceiver. This hardware platform was extended during the following years with the following chip generations:

- Series 100 (2003)
- Series 200 (2005)
- Series 300 (2007)
- Series 400 (2009)
- Series 500 (2013)
- Series 700 (2018).

Figure 1.8 shows the current workhorse, the Series 500 IC. The ASIC combines the radio transceiver, a microcontroller, embedded memory, and quite a few peripheral components in one single chip. Most of the Z-Wave products sold today just use this chip to implement all functions. This is a huge cost and complexity saving compared to discrete implementation where controller, memory, I/Os, and radio transceivers are separate components. The chapter 6.3 gives further information about the ASIC and the way it is used in products.

Besides, the ASIC Silicon Labs also provides a system development kit (SDK) to simplify the product development. This contains, among other things, precompiled libraries for various applications covering all aspects of the communication protocol.

Figure 1.8: Silicon Labs Z-Wave ASIC Series 500 keys granted (Source: Silicon Labs)

All manufacturers are required to use one of these libraries for their product development, leading to similar behavior of all Z-Wave devices on the lower protocol layers. Z-Wave also defines application-specific functions (e.g. switch A is turned on when button B is pressed), but the manufacturers are responsible to implement this. Most manufacturers optimize and enhance functions on the application layer.

Hence, the Z-Wave product certification process focuses mainly on application layer functions to ensure that different devices from different manufacturers work together seamlessly.

1.6.3   Z-Wave becomes an open standard

Initially, Z-Wave started as a proprietary system available only to those manufacturers who agreed to design products based on Zensys technology.

With the adoption of the Z-Wave technology in the market and the increasing success of Z-Wave as an interoperable ecosystem of devices, the technology was more and more opened up.

The first step into this direction was certainly the incorporation of the Z-Wave Alliance, which now acts as the central marketing engine and collection of vendors. As of 2016, more than 450 different companies from all parts of the world have joined the Alliance. An interesting aspect is the broad diversity of the Al-

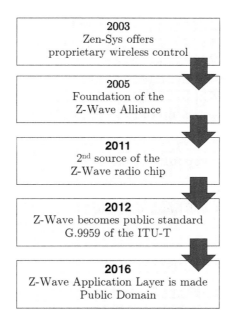

Figure 1.9: Evolution from proprietary solution to public standard

liance. World market leaders are found beside small startups and companies from different backgrounds such as security, marketing, light switches, plastic molding, TV, remote control business, software, test house, etc. are all lined up in support of this interoperable standard.

The next step in opening up the Z-Wave world was the availability of a second source for the Z-Wave SOC chip. In 2011, Japanese company Mitsumi announced the availability of a certified SOC from its factories. [Mitsumi2011]

In 2012, the Z-Wave radio layer was made the open and public standard G.9959 by the International Telecommunication Union (ITU-T). [ITU2012] In 2016, Sigma Designs and the Z-Wave Alliance decided to open up the application layer specification that is now available free of charge to the public at

```
http://zwavepublic.com/
```

This website also offers open-source example code for controllers and ready-to-use software, e.g. for the Raspberry Pi platform [Sigma2016].

1.6.4   Z-Wave Plus

In 2013, the Z-Wave Alliance released a significant enhancement of the Z-Wave standard called **Z-Wave Plus**.

The objective of the Z-Wave Plus is to further simplify the use of Z-Wave and to enhance the user experience with Z-Wave devices. Z-Wave networks can be installed without technical knowledge, and in most cases, even without reading the devices manual. Also, the Z-Wave Plus reflects the changes that have happened in the smart home market since it first hit the market. Fifteen years ago, smart home installations were primarily operated by wall controllers and remote controls. Now the primary interface to the smart home is the smartphone or tablet.

Hence, the Z-Wave Plus extends the existing specifications by narrowing down to some of the options and freedom manufacturers had before. At the same time, it introduces some new functionalities that are particularly tailored to simplify operation by graphical user interfaces such as phones and pads communicating with IP to a central controller, also referred to as IP gateway. Most of the new limitations are essentially "best practice" that were used in the devices anyway but now become mandatory so that other devices can rely on these behaviors. This simplifies the design of central controllers and user interfaces for configuration and use of the network. One of the new features is that Z-Wave devices are now required to provide more information about themselves wirelessly to eliminate the need to consult the manual for a lot of configuration tasks.

Z-Wave Plus devices are tested by a new certification process which was substantially extended compared to the old interoperability testing.

Besides interoperability as the core and primary purpose of the Z-Wave certification program, additional parts of the manual and the product description are checked too.

Figure 1.6.4 shows the new Z-Wave Plus logo, which indicates that the given device complies with the tighter rules of Z-Wave Plus.

The key elements of Z-Wave Plus are:

1. Precise definition of the devices roles in the Z-Wave network. Further information about this can be found in Chapter 3.3.3.

2. Precise definition of possible Z-Wave device types. Further information about this can be found in Chapter 4.1.4.

3. The lifeline concept. Further information about this can be found in Chapter 4.2.7.

4. Extension of the certification program to cover manuals, product packaging, use of logos

Figure 1.10: Z-Wave Plus Logo

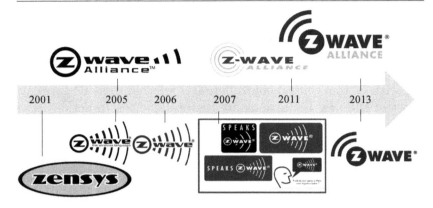

Figure 1.11: Z-Wave Logo evolution

5. Z-Wave Plus devices require the use of a
   modern Series 500 ASIC providing 150 % faster communication, higher wireless reliability, and lower battery power
   consumption.

All Z-Wave Plus devices are 100% compatible with standard Z-
Wave devices, now called Z-Wave classic.

1.6.5   How to recognize Z-Wave

While Z-Wave has shown a remarkable stability in terms of technology and backward compatibility, its marketing efforts were
not equally consistent. Figure 1.11 shows the evolution of the
Z-Wave logo from Zensys's initial design to a modern look and
feel which has been in use for quite a few years now.

Chapter 2

Radio Layer

2.1   Wireless Basics

In an ideal situation, radio waves spread steadily like light waves in all directions, generating a spherical field. For technical applications, the wavelength (λ) and the frequency (f) are related to each other with the formula:

$$\lambda = \frac{c}{f}$$

- λ: Wavelength in km
- c: Light speed = 300.000 km/s
- f: Frequency in Hz

In contrast to infrared light or light waves in general, radio waves can penetrate walls, furniture, and other objects. Such obstacles, however, weaken the radio signal and reduce the range.

If wireless components are installed, it is recommended to remove as many obstacles as possible between the wireless transmitter and the receiver. In practice, this means that wireless components should not be installed in random places. The ability of radio signals to penetrate walls and other obstacles depends on

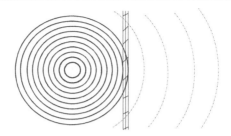

Figure 2.1: Attenuation of radio signals by a wall

the frequency of the signal. Generally, radio frequencies below 1 GHz have a higher ability to penetrate walls than, e.g. signals in the 2.4 GHz, a frequency used by commonly known technologies such as WLAN or ZigBee. Figure 2.1 illustrates the attenuation of radio signals by a wall.

The central parameter to deal with in wireless transmission is "wireless energy." There is a certain wireless energy transmitted by the sender and there is a certain (minimum) energy received by the receiver. For transmitters, the most important measure is the so-called effective radiated power (ERP). This is essentially the total amount of energy released by the antenna and a measure of how well the transmitter and its antenna are working. The emitted energy is measured in Watt. Unfortunately, Watt values are hard to calculate since they may change by several orders of magnitude (i.e. 10, 100, 1000 times). To make calculations simpler, engineers use a logarithmic measure (to the base of 10) in db and normalize this to 1 mW. This means that the statement "this transmitter sends 0dBm" equals to "this transmitter sends with 1 mW." Other energy values are defined in plus or minus dbm where 10 db is a factor of 10.

- 10 mW is +10 dBm
- 100 mW is + 20 dBm
- 0.1 mW is - 10 dBm

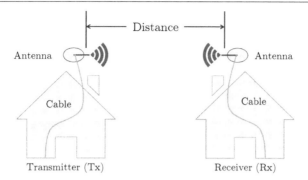

Figure 2.2: Model's transmission path between sender and receiver

- 25 mW (the maximum allowed emission of SRD bands) is 14 dBm

One rule of thumb is

- double the emitted energy is + 3 dBm
- cut the emitted energy in half is - 3bBm

As we will see, this logarithmic measure is useful for calculations on wireless range and wireless attenuation.

2.2 Frequencies used by Z-Wave

Wireless systems are restricted in the use of their frequencies. International regulations limit smart home devices to few frequency areas. The most popular of them is the so-called 2.4 GHz band, used by Wi-Fi or Bluetooth, among others. The big advantage of the 2.4 GHz frequency band is that it is globally available so manufacturers can supply one single product to the whole world. However, the success of the 2.4 GHz band has now turned into its biggest disadvantage. The frequencies are highly congested. Tradeshows and hotels where Wi-Fi sometimes does not work

Figure 2.3: ITU Region Split of the World (Source: Wikipedia, under CC BY-SA 2.5)

anymore due to heavy congestion are only the tip of the iceberg. Multiple Wi-Fi devices per home, meanwhile, turn apartment complexes into a similar situation and the deployment of many more Wi-Fi-based smart home devices will only accelerate the congestion process even further.

Z-Wave has therefore chosen frequencies below the 1 GHz level. They are not as congested as 2.4 GHz and provide an about 50 % better range at same transmission power. However this advantage comes at its price too. There is no globally available frequency below the 1 GHz barrier [1].

The International Telecommunication Union (ITU), in its International Radio Regulations, has divided the world into three ITU regions in order to manage the global radio spectrum. Each region has its own set of frequency allocations, the main reason for defining the regions. Figure 2.3 shows the regions. The area on the left hand side indicates Region 1, the part around Africa and

---

[1]Of course, there are other frequency areas way below 1 GHz which can be used globally, but they are not suited for smart home for technical reasons such as antenna size, range, etc.

Figure 2.4: Members of the CEPT-Organization in Europe keys granted (Source: Wikipedia)

Europe indicates Region 2, and the right hand side Region 3.

The frequency band below 1 GHz dedicated to applications like smart home control is called Industry Science Medicine (ISM). It ranges from 902 MHz to 930 MHz, with a center frequency of 915 MHz. Unfortunately, this band is only available in Region 1 countries and in some dedicated countries of Region 3 such as Australia, New Zealand, and Taiwan. All Region 2 countries and the bulk of Region 3 countries such as China use the much smaller and even higher regulated Short Range Device frequency band ranging from 865 to 870 MHz, also called SRD 860.

2.2.1 SRD 860

The SRD 860 band ranges from 865 MHz to 870 MHz. Since it is much smaller than the ISM band, the regulators expect more use and have therefore applied additional regulations of the frequency band. Most importantly, they have divided the band into sub-bands, where different maximum emission limits apply and other

Frequency	Duty cycle	ERP
863-865 MHz	100% (wireless audio)	10 mW
863.0 - 865.6 MHz	0.1% or LBT+AFA	25 mW
865.0 - 868.0 MHz	1% or LBT+AFA	25 mW
868.0 - 868.6 MHz	1% or LBT+AFA	25 mW
868.7 - 869.2 MHz	0.1% or LBT+AFA	25 mW
869.4 - 869.65 MHz	10% or LBT+AFA, 25 kHz channel spacing	500 mW
869.7 - 870.0 MHz	100% (voice communication)	5 mW

Table 2.1: Structure of the frequency band

technologies must be used to reduce interference and congestion. Table 2.1 shows the structure of the sub-bands.

All countries of ITU Region 2 and the better part of ITU Region 3 grant this frequency band to Z-Wave, but different countries assign different frequencies.

Fortunately, there is one large group of countries gathered in the CEPT organization.

> **"The European Conference of Postal and Telecommunications Administrations (CEPT) was established on June 26, 1959, as a coordinating body for European state telecommunications and postal organizations. The acronym comes from the French version of its name 'Conference europenne des administrations des postes et des telecommunications.' CEPT was responsible for the creation of the European Telecommunications Standards Institute** (ETSI) **in 1988.** [CEPT2017]"

Figure 2.4 shows the members of the CEPT. All the members agreed to grant the two frequencies 868.4 MHz and 869.85 MHz to Z-Wave. Only India and Russia picked different frequencies.

The SRD 860 band has a list of restrictions to ensure minimal interference:

- The **Duty-Cycle** defines the ratio of the timeslot the transmitter is sending out a signal of a given frequency and the timeslot the transmitter has to stay quiet (not sending a signal) right after the transmission. The purpose of this constraint is to ensure a fair use of the frequency by multiple transmitters. One transmitter will not block the frequency for too long a time.

- The technology **Listen Before Talk (LBT)** defines that a transmitter will always listen on the frequency given to detect that no other transmitter is actually sending out signals. This cannot eliminate but does reduce the amount of collisions where two transmitters send on the same frequency at the same time and jam the signal.

- The technology **Adaptive Frequency Agility (AFA)** describes how different frequencies are used to transmit certain information.

- The emitted wireless power is also limited. The regulation defines a maximum **ERP** (*Emitted Radio Power*) per subfrequency range. Most parts of the SRD frequency band are limited to 25 mW or +8 dBm.

2.2.2   ISM 915

The ISM band 902–930 Mhz is defined by the ITU Radio Regulations (Article 6) in footnotes 5.138, 5.150, and 5.280 of the Radio Regulations. All countries in ITU Region 1 and some countries in ITU Region 3 assign this frequency band to Z-Wave. However, the real frequency within this band differs from country to country. In the United States, the use of the ISM band is governed by Part 15 of the Federal Communications Commission (FCC) rules.

Figure 2.5: FCC Logo

Within these rules, Z-Wave uses the frequencies of 908.40 MHz and 916.00 MHz. Most of the countries in the region mentioned follow the US regulation and assign the very same frequencies, so that devices from the United States can be used there at least from the frequency point of view. Another large group of countries, namely Australia, Brasil, Peru, Paraguay, and Hong Kong, use the frequency pair of 919,80 Mhz and 921,04 MHz. Some other countries use other frequencies.

FCC does not limit the ERP but only allows 50 mV/m of electrical field strength at 3-meter distance. This roughly translates into an ERP of -1 dBm. Other regulations like duty cycle do not apply. Figure 2.5 shows the FCC label indicating compliance with these regulations.

2.2.3 How Z-Wave with different frequencies

Annex D shows the different frequencies in different countries and the underlying national or international specifications.

Z-Wave ICs can be tuned in to any of the frequencies mentioned just by setting certain configuration values during production. Some Z-Wave controllers such as the leading DIY gateway RaZberry even allow switching the frequencies, as shown in Figure 2.6. However, there is a problem: To avoid sideband emissions and to filter incoming signals from the antenna, Z-Wave ICs require an antenna filter, also called SAW filter. This filter only

Figure 2.6: Screenshot of Z-Way User Interface for Frequency Switching (Source: Expert User Interface of Z-Way by Z-Wave.Me)

Marker	E	A	U
Frequency	865-870 MHz	919-926 MHz	908-916 MHz
Examples	Europe, China, Russia, India	Australia, Brasil, Japan	USA, Israel, Mexico

Table 2.2: Saw Filter and Frequency Restrictions

allows a certain portion of the frequency spectrum to pass and blocks all other frequencies from leaving the antenna and being received from the antenna.

This means that all specific Z-Wave frequencies need their own specific SAW filter. Fortunately, the frequencies countries have approved can be grouped into three groups around the center frequencies of 868 MHz, 910 MHz, and 920 MHz. These three SAW filter types are sufficient to support all countries worldwide. Silicon Labs offers modules combining the Z-Wave ASIC with the SAW filter for easier integration. The SAW filter is marked on the Z-Wave modules (e.g. ZM5202, a component with Z-Wave chip plus SAW filter) with the letters 'E' (868MHz), 'U' (910 MHz), and 'A' (920MHz). Table 2.2 summarizes the labels, the frequency range supported, and their most important countries. Image 2.7 shows an example of the marking on the Z-Wave module.

2.3 Wireless Range Estimations

There is substantial theory behind the radiation of radio signals. The basic challenge is to ensure that enough energy from the sender is transmitted to the receiver. Figure 2.2 shows the basic transmission path with the various components impacting the wireless range.

Figure 2.7: ZM5202 Module with Filter identifier (arrow) (Source: Silicon Labs)

To estimate the wireless range of a wireless system, the following information must be available:

- ERP of the transmitter.
- Loss of the cable from transmitter to antenna.
- Loss of the transmitter antenna.
- Path Loss.
- Loss of the receiver antenna.
- Loss of the cable from Antenna to Receiver.
- Sensitivity of the Receiver.

The loss on the connection cables can usually be ignored since the antenna is typically quite close to the receiver or transmitter.

The **Path Loss** is the reduction in power density that occurs as a radio wave propagates over a distance. Radio waves follow an inverse square law for power density: The power density is proportional to the inverse square of the distance. Every time the distance is doubled, only one-fourth of the power is received. This means that every 6 dBm increase in output power doubles the possible distance that is achievable.

Besides transmitter power, another factor affecting the range is the receiver sensitivity. It is usually expressed in dBm as well.

Since both output power and receiver sensitivity are stated in dBm, you can use simple addition and subtraction to calculate the maximum path loss that a system can incur:

$$MaximumPathLoss = transmitpower - receiversensitivity$$

The path loss also depends on the frequency used. Higher frequencies will result in a decrease in the wireless range. While the calculation model of the radio transmission is quite complex, there is a simplified equation to estimate the wireless range as a function of the frequency and the maximum path loss.

$$s = 10^{\frac{pl - 32,44 - 20*log(f)}{20}}$$

- s: Distance in Kilometer
- pl: Maximum path loss in dBm
- f: Frequency in MHz

Let's apply this to the Z-Wave situation. The datasheet of the Silicon Labs transceiver ZM5101 [Sigma2013] reveals a maximum transmitter power of +1 dBm and a maximum receiver sensitivity of -102 dBm. Using the equation above, this results in a maximum range of 3.8 km for Z-Wave. Unfortunately, this is just a theoretical value. Real communication links do not even get close to this for various reasons.

The **Link-Margin** is another parameter to describe the relationship between emitted resp. received energy and distance. In case a distance between sender and receiver and the emitted energy resp. the receiver's sensitivity are given, the link margin describes the buffer in dBm. The emitted energy could drop, still ensuring a stable wireless connection.

Assuming a distance between sender and receiver of 100 m, the path loss of this distance is -72 dBm. Applying the situation in Z-Wave with a maximum possible path loss of 102 dBm, the link margin for the two devices 100 meters away is 102 dBm -72 dBm = 30 dBm.

2.3.1   Background Noise

The air is polluted with energy emitted by various transceivers. Therefore, it is not enough that the wireless signal of one certain transmitter just reaches the receiver. It must transport more energy than other transmitters emitting on the same frequency. The limiting factor is the background noise, which is referred to as noise floor. This is the level of energy that constantly comes from various other emitting sources. Sources of this energy are other devices using the same frequency band or sideband emissions of other transmitters or electrical gear. For example, in Europe the LTE service (4G mobile data) sometimes uses the 852 MHz band and sideband missions reach the 868 MHz band used in Z-Wave. Other sources of wireless noise can be:

- Computers.
- Microwave devices.
- Electronic transformers.
- Audio equipment and video equipment.
- Pre-coupling devices for fluorescent lamps.
- Disturbances by switch of electric motors and other inductive loads.
- Interference by defective electrical appliances.
- Disturbances by HF welding apparatuses.
- Medical treatment devices.

Figure 2.8 shows a viewgraph of the background noise on the two frequencies used by Z-Wave, as provided by the **Certified Installer Toolkit (CIT)**, a special tool available to Z-Wave installers for network debugging. For more information about the CIT, please refer to Chapter 5.3. There is a measured general noise level of about -90 dBm. Even if the Z-Wave receiver has a much higher sensitivity, this will not help to extend the wireless range due to this background noise.

The background noise will reduce the total link margin from 1-(-102)=103 dBm down to 1-(-90) = 91 dBm, resulting in a possible maximum range of about 300 m.

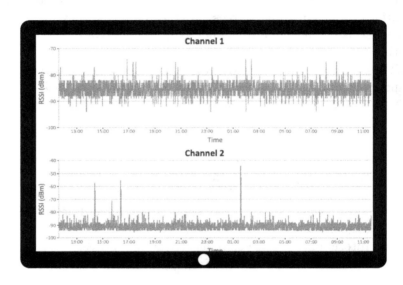

Figure 2.8: Background Noise (Source: Certified Installer Toolkit User Interface)

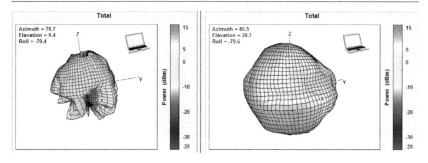

Figure 2.9: Comparison of two Antenna Designs (Source: Z-Wave Europe GmbH)

2.3.2   Antenna Design and Antenna Loss

It is certainly possible to build an antenna that does not have any loss. However, most antennas of Z-Wave devices have to fit into small devices or need to meet other design criteria. That is why a good portion of the energy is lost right at the antenna. On the other hand, antennas can also generate a gain. The equations assume an isotropic (perfect round) antenna without any preferred direction. Real-world antennas do not work equally well in all directions and may therefore generate a gain in certain directions at the expense of even higher loss in other directions. Antennas for Z-Wave devices will have no preferred direction, which is why it is not realistic to expect any relevant antenna gain. Figure 2.9 shows the characteristics of two Z-Wave antennas as measured in a professional antenna test laboratory. The antenna shown on the left side may work well in certain directions and may fail completely in other directions. The right side shows a very good antenna design.

Figure 2.10 shows the dramatic impact of a bad antenna design or bad antenna position. The antenna under test is a standard helix antenna used in many Z-Wave USB sticks. On the left-

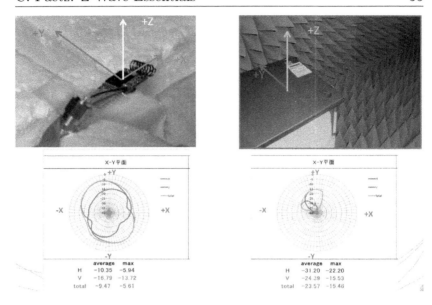

Figure 2.10: Performance of a standard Helix antenna, antenna can be seen on the left hand side (Source: Mitsumi Semiconductors)

hand side, the stick works quite well, still resulting in an antenna loss of almost 10 dBm. This may sound large but is not unusual for this type of small antenna. The right-hand side shows the same product with the same antenna, but here the USB stick is connected right into the USB slot of a PC. The large metal structure in proximity to the helix antenna has a big impact: The antenna loss is now -23 dBm with some directions where the antenna will completely fail.

Besides the helix antenna used in this case, there are a few more commonly used antenna designs on the market. Best results can certainly be achieved with a dedicated 800–900 MHz antenna. Unfortunately, they are bulky and expensive but a good choice for industrial applications. Figure 2.11 shows such a dedicated

Figure 2.11: Dedicated Z-Wave Antenna on an industrial Z-Wave Gateway

Z-Wave antenna on an industrial Z-Wave Gateway.

Very often a simple wire, also called whip antenna, of a defined length of $\lambda/4$ is used in Z-Wave devices, as shown in Figure 2.12. If trimmed to the right size, these antennas can work reasonably well, but there is the danger that end users might bend them resulting in severe loss of performance.

Therefore, the simplest way to implement an antenna is to use a piece of copper or trace on the printed circuit board, a PCBA antenna. This sort of antenna can be seen in Figure 2.13. If done well, the antenna can have the same or even better performance than an external wire but will not reach the performance of a dedicated external antenna.

2.3.3 Attenuation

The radio signal is further attenuated by obstacles between the sender and the receiver. Whenever there is an obstacle in the direct line of sight between the transmitter and receiver, the resulting distance is shorter than the maximum distance achievable with the given antenna. The attenuation depends on the material of the obstacle and the corresponding ability of the radio

Figure 2.12: Dedicated wire as Z-Wave antenna (Source: Philio Technology Corporation, Inc.)

Figure 2.13: PCBA Antenna (Source: Z-Wave Europe GmbH)

Nr.	Material	Thickness	Attenuation
2	Plaster	< 10 cm	10 %
3	Glass (without metal coating)	< 5 cm	10 %
4	Stone	< 30 cm	30 %
5	Pumice	< 30 cm	10 %
6	Aerated concrete stone	< 30 cm	20 %
7	Red brick	< 30 cm	35 %
8	Iron-reinforced concrete	< 30 cm	30 ...90 %
9	Ceiling	< 30 cm	70 %
10	Outer wall	< 30 cm	60 %
11	Inner wall	< 30 cm	40 %
12	Metal grid	< 1 mm	90 %
13	Aluminum coating	< 1 mm	100 %

Table 2.3: Attenuation of different material [Merten2008]

frequency to penetrate this material.

Table 2.3 shows the percentage attenuation of a radio signal depending on the material using a typical thickness of this material. These factors allow calculating the typical maximum radio distance between transmitter and receiver using the schema given in Table 2.4.

If the radio signal penetrates the obstacle at a bleak angle (other than 90 degrees), then the attenuation effect will increase.

The locations of transmitter and receiver should, therefore, be selected in such a way that the direct connecting line only runs on a very short distance through the material that causes attenuation. Figure 2.14 demonstrates the effective wall thickness.

If the calculated range of the attenuated signal is longer than the measured distance between transmitter and receiver, the components should function well. Pieces of furniture, device mounting, metal coatings, and plantings should all be considered when planning the best route for your wireless system. Because these

Obstacle	Act. Distance	Type	Attenuation	New distance
No 1	30 m	Concrete	30%	21 m
Take new value to next step				
No 2	21 m	Glass	10%	18,90 m
Take new value to next step				
No 3	18,9 m	Plaster wall	10%	17 m
Take new value to next step				
..	17 m	..	..	..

Table 2.4: Work Sheet to determine the wireless distance

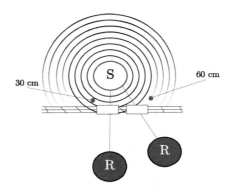

Figure 2.14: Effective wall thickness

attenuations are approximate, a test is recommended before the fixed installation is made.

For most estimations of wireless range such as on data sheets, the attenuation by obstacles is not taken into account. The estimation of the wireless range for Z-Wave assumes a free line of sight.

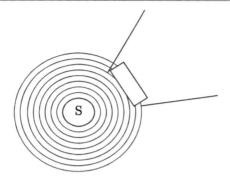

Figure 2.15: Radio shadow by metallic structures

2.3.4   Wireless Shadows

Metallic parts of the building or pieces of furniture shield the electromagnetic waves. Behind such a structure there may be the so-called radio shadow as shown in Figure 2.15. No direct reception is possible.

Despite radio shadow, it is possible for wireless signals to be reflected by metal structures and still reach the final destination. Reflections are unpredictable, and it is recommended that you test your systems before permanent installation.

2.3.5   Reflections and Interference

Reflections are used by amateur radio connections to bridge big distances (several thousand kilometers with relatively low power) in the short-wave band. In this case, the reflective property of the ionosphere is used. Within buildings, reflections may cause disturbances or attenuation if the original and the reflected way are received together. The receipt of the original transmission and one or more of its reflections is commonly referred to as **multi-path** as the signals travel by multiple paths on their way

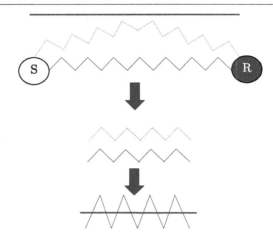

Figure 2.16: Signal gain by constructive or in-phase interference

to the receiver.

Figure 2.16 illustrates the signal gain by interference. Interference can occur in different phase situations that are caused by different run times and by the way the radio waves are increased or attenuated.

Figure 2.17 shows the signal attenuation by destructive interference. Interference can be resolved by slightly changing the positions of the transmitter or receiver. Even a couple of millimeters may work. Sometimes it is a process of trial and error to see what works for you in your home.

2.3.6   Fade Margin

Reflections in the environment surrounding a transmitter and receiver create multiple paths that a transmitted signal can traverse. Thus, the receiver sees the superposition of multiple copies of the transmitted signal, each traversing a different path. Each signal copy will experience differences in attenuation, delay, and

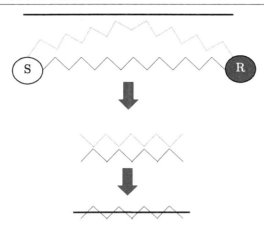

Figure 2.17: Signal attenuation by destructive or out-of-phase interference

phase shift while travelling from the source to the receiver. As just shown, this can result in either constructive or destructive interference, amplifying or attenuating the signal power seen at the receiver. Strong destructive interference is frequently referred to as a deep fade and may result in temporary failure of communication due to a severe drop in the channel signal-to-noise ratio. Since these reflections, etc. also depend on constantly changing environmental conditions such as ionization of the air, humidity, etc., the reception of the signals will always change. Hence, the change is called **Fading** and the maximum acceptable hange of signal strength is referred to as **Fade Margin**.

Figure 2.18 shows the signal strength of a series of communications between two nodes at fixed positions. The measured signal strength varies from -64 to -68 dBm. When measuring the link quality, Z-Wave assumes a fade margin of 6 dBm to ensure that the link remains stable even under bad conditions.

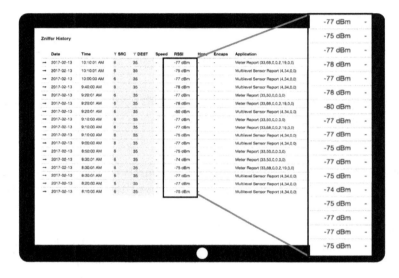

Figure 2.18: Signal Strength Fading of Link between two nodes
(Source: Certified Installer Toolkit CIT, z-wavealliance.org)

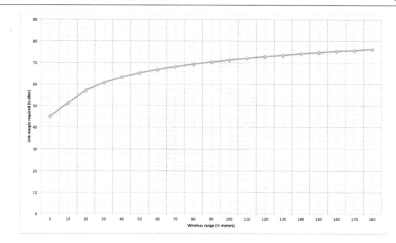

Figure 2.19: Wireless Range versus Link Margin

2.3.7   Summary

Figure 2.19 shows the required link margin to reach a certain wireless distance. Applying the Z-Wave ZM5101 IC parameters for transmission (+1 dBm), a typical antenna loss of 15 dBm, reception above noise (-90 dBm), and a safety margin of 6 dBm, we can assume a safe wireless range of 41 m. This matches the testing conditions of Z-Wave devices. During certification, they must bridge a distance of 40 m in-house without major errors.

2.4   Electro Magnetic Energy (EME) and Health

From infrared, to Bluetooth, to Z-Wave, there are numerous wireless messages flying through the air. There is a general concern whether or not wireless radio transmissions can affect users health. The most critical factor is the energy entry into the hu-

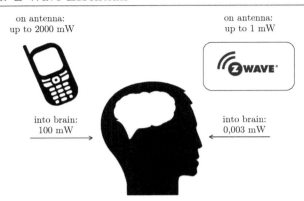

Figure 2.20: Transmitting power of Z-Wave compared to cell phone

man brain. To get an idea about the effect of certain wireless signals to the human body, it makes sense to look at the conventional mobile phone as a reference. Mobile phones transmit a constant radio signal with a peak energy level of 2000 mW into the brain when held next to the ear. Without any other protection and mostly operating next to the ear, a person will absorb about 100 mW of energy into his head. This exposure continues throughout the whole telephone call! Z-Wave presents nowhere near such a threat as mobile phones. Z-Wave works with peak transmission powers of max. 10mW and this power level is only applied for 1 % of the time (duty cycle = 1 %). This corresponds to an average radiation power of only 0.1 mW. In addition to this much lower radiated power, it is rare that a Z-Wave transmitter, e.g. a remote control or motion detector, operates directly in or close to the body.

Figure 2.20 shows the direct comparison between the transmitting power of Z-Wave and a cell phone.

The signal attenuation that is generated in 1m distance. This causes another reduction in the radiation power around the factor of 40. The human body is only hit by a radiation power of 0.025 mW. This is about 1:4000 lower than the emission of a mobile phone. Also considering that the radio signal will only be transmitted during a short period of time when a button is pressed or a sensor signal is transmitted, the electromagnetic emission of a Z-Wave network does not contribute to the general electromagnetic pollution in a home and does not have any negative effect on human beings.

Chapter 3

Z-Wave Networking

3.1 Data Communication with G.9959

Z-Wave uses its designated frequencies in the SRD frequency band in a standardized way. This standard is issued by the ITU-T under the number G.9959 [ITU2012]. It uses two terms to describe the communication:

- The **Physical layer (PHY)** defines the way the frequency is used and how certain bits are encoded and transmitted.
- The **Media access control (MAC)** defines how a whole data stream can be transported from one device to another via the wireless link.

3.1.1 The PHY function

The PHY function defines how to transport bits from a transmitter to a receiver. Z-Wave is not bound to a certain frequency, but it uses the recommended frequencies defined in Chapter 2.2.3. Depending on the frequencies, different line encodings and line speeds are used.

In general, Z-Wave uses three **Channels**. They differ in terms of data rate, modulation, and frequency used. The reason for this

Channel	1	at 2	at 2
Data Rate	9.6 kB/s	40 kB/s	100 kB/s
Encoding	Manchester	NRZ	NRZ
Frequency	Frequency 1 (e.g. 868.4 MHz or 908.4 MHz)	Frequency 2	Frequency B (e.g. 869.85 MHz or 916 MHz)

Table 3.1: Z-Wave Channels

is that Z-Wave can switch the frequency if one frequency is congested. The different data enable a fallback since lower data rate generally means more robust communication. The channel used is negotiated between every two communicating nodes while the channel with the slowest data rate is the least common denominator. This means that one device may communicate with different channels to different devices. The three channels of Z-Wave are described in Table 3.1

Z-Wave uses frequency shift keying, also referred to as FSK. To encode bits, a logical "0" is transmitted by sending a signal on one frequency and a logical "1" is transmitted using a different frequency. The Z-Wave transmitter either sends on frequency A or on frequency B or does not send at all. The difference between the two frequencies is 20 KHz. In case of the CEPT frequency, the real frequencies used for transmission are either 868.40 MHz or 868.42 MHz for communication in Channels 1 and 2 (9.6 kbit/s and 40 kbit/s). For communication in Channel 3 (100 kbit/s data rate), the frequency difference is 29.4 kHz. This results in two frequencies of 869.85 MHz and 870.14 MHz.

The frequency difference for FSK is a tradeoff between two goals. The two frequencies shall be far enough away from each other to make sure that a receiver can easily distinguish a "0" from a "1" in a noisy environment. On the other hand, they need to be close enough to make sure that one single antenna filter (designed for

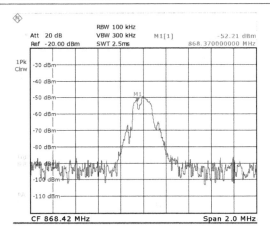

Figure 3.1: Frequency Spectrum

the frequency in the middle between the two frequencies) is not attenuating the two signals for "0" and "1" too much.

Figure 3.1 shows a measured frequency spectrum of a Z-Wave transmitter under real conditions with background noise. As can be seen, it is everything but simple to filter real "0" and "1" out of such a spectrum. The receiving part of the Z-Wave link needs to apply certain filters to find the right frequencies and to decode the data that was sent.

Historically, Z-Wave used a data rate of 9.6 kbit/s. Since this is more than sufficient for small commands like turning on or off a switch, more complicated functions like firmware updating or transmission of metering values need a higher data rate.

In later versions of the Z-Wave protocol, a 40 kbit/s data rate was added to the protocol. Modern implementations are based on the Series 500 ICs and beyond a third transmission mode of 100 kb/s with a dedicated frequency.

To differentiate between the two data rates of 9.6 kbit/s and 40

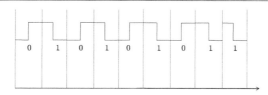

Figure 3.2: Manchester-Encoding

kbit/s, sharing the same frequency Z-Wave defines different line encodings.

The different data rates use a different way how a "0" and a "1" is encoded. In order to allow a reliable transmission of bits, the encodings need to meet the following two criteria:

- The '0' and the '1' need to be reasonably different to differentiate them from one another.
- The encoding needs to ensure that the received data allows to recover the sending clock rate to differentiate the bits following each other.

Manchester Encoding   The 9.6 kbit/s data uses the so-called Manchester encoding. The transmitting time is structured in steps and in the middle of each step the frequency changes. A change from higher to lower frequency encodes a '1', from the lower to the higher frequency a '0'. A frequency change right on the border of the step does not represent an encoded data but is needed to encode to similar bits after another. Figure 3.2 shows a typical pattern of Manchester encoding.

Non Return Zero   The 40 kB/s and the 100 kB/s data rates use the so-called non-return zero or NRZ encoding. One frequency represents a "1" and the other frequency represents the "0." Figure 3.3 shows a typical pattern of NRZ encoding.

Both encodings have their advantages and disadvantages. The

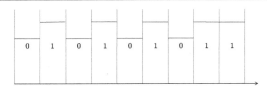

Figure 3.3: NRZ-Encoding

Manchester encoding ensures that there are many changes in frequencies that can be used to recover the original data clock. On the other hand, sequences with many similar bits (like 0x0ffff or 0x0000) result in doubling the frequency of the frequency change. NRZ reduces the amount of frequency changes, but sequences of similar bits make the recovery of data clock more difficult. Both encodings are frequently used for data communication and both are well suited for communication in smart homes.

3.1.2 Wireless Frame (MAC-Frame)

In order to allow the receiver to find the right 0s and 1s, the transmitter needs to send a well-known pattern prior to the actual data. This so-called "preamble" is used to synchronize the receiver with the transmitter. The preamble is a sequence of 0-1-0-1-0-1-0-1 that is repeated a minimum of 10 times.

After the preamble, there is the so-called **start of frame delimiter**. This byte signals that the data part of the frame is starting. After the actual data is sent, the whole communication is concluded with an **end of frame delimiter** of one byte.

Figure 3.4 shows the basic MAC frame as defined in ITU-T G.9959 res. Z-Wave. The maximum user data size is 64 bytes. Later in this chapter and in Chapter 4, it is explained that the minimum user data size is 12 bytes. This allows some calculation:

The total frame size including preamble, data, start

Preample	SOF	Byte 1 ... N	EOF

Preample: 10 * 01010101b to synchronize
SOF: Start of Frame, 1 Byte
EOF: End of Frame, 1 Byte

Figure 3.4: Z-Wave (PHY/MAC) Wireless Frame

Speed	at 9.6 kbit/s	at 40 kbit/s	at 100 kbit/s
Channel	1	2	3
25 bytes	20 ms	5 ms	2 ms
76 bytes	63 ms	15 ms	6 ms

Table 3.2: Transmission times of minimal and maximal PHY frames

> of frame delimiter and end of frame delimiter is 10
> bytes + 1 byte + 12 bytes ... 64 bytes + 1 byte = 24
> bytes ... 76 bytes.

Table 3.2 shows the different times needed to transmit Z-Wave frames with the different frequencies.

3.1.3   Home-ID and Node-ID

A wireless communication network needs to make sure that certain information is transported from the right sender to the right receiver. This means that a receiver needs to be able to find out

- what data elements are to be received and
- what data elements are not addressed to it and should be ignored.

The second point is particularly important if multiple wireless networks are operated within the same physical location. As soon as different networks overlap (e.g. in houses or apartments that are close to each other), the wireless network protocol needs to make sure that the data stays within the originating network and is only received by a receiver that is also a member of the network. All data of foreign networks must be rejected. Within a single network, the wireless protocol needs to ensure that the specific receiver of a data message knows that this message is for him and not for a different device in the same network. In order to accomplish both tasks, the general rule in a network is:

> **All devices in a network need to have *something* in common and they need to have *something* that is individual for each and every device.**

In wired networks the *something in common* is typically the access to the same wire. All devices connected to this wire belong to the same network. In the wireless world, there is no wire. There are two different ways to solve the problem:

- Every device has a unique identifier. This identifier is assigned at the time of manufacturing.
- Only "master" or "inclusion" devices have a unique identifier assigned to them at the time of manufacture. All other devices are shipped "dumb" and receive their identifier during a pairing process.

In a technology that uses unique addresses, each device that ever gets manufactured needs to have one single unique numerical ID to distinguish it from all other devices in existence. An example of this is Wi-Fi. The unique address is here referred to a MAC address and can be found on every Wi-Fi router or other Wi-Fi devices. The advantage of this approach is that the network management can never fail and devices can always be distinguished from other devices in the same or another network. The price for this approach is that every device in a network needs to maintain a list of the addresses of all other devices in the same network. This consumes memory and may take computing power if the list gets long and needs to be searched.

Therefore, Z-Wave has chosen a different way. Only master or "inclusion" devices have unique identifiers. All other devices are empty or "dumb." When a master or "inclusion" controller creates a network, it shares its unique identifier with the dumb device and this becomes the network ID or the element that all devices in this network will have in common. The master or "inclusion" controller also assigns a sequential device or Node-ID so that each individual device within the same network can have identified addresses during the inclusion of a device into the network.

This has advantages and disadvantages:

- A clear advantage is less need of memory and a much simpler addressing and address filtering.
- The disadvantage is that, in case the controller does something wrong, there may be two devices with similar addresses in one network creating confusion.

The Z-Wave protocol defines two identifications for the organization of the network:

- The **Home-ID** is the common identification of all nodes belonging to one logical Z-Wave network. It has a length of 4 bytes = 32 bits.
- The **Node-ID** is the address of the single node [1] within the network. The Node-ID has a length of 1 byte = 8 bits. Since a few Node-IDs are reserved for internal network organization functions, Z-Wave allows addressing 232 different nodes within one wireless network.

Nodes of different Home-IDs do not belong to the same network and cannot communicate with each other. Its therefore not a problem to have more than one device with the same Node-ID in one room as long as they have different Home-IDs and thus belong to different networks.

Certain Z-Wave devices are called controllers because they can

---

[1]Devices in a network are also referred to as nodes. Since the term "Node-ID" used this wording, all devices will be referred to here as nodes as well.

assign their own Home-IDs to other nodes and also assign a network-wide individual Node-ID to the same node. All other devices are called slaves because they cannot assign a Home-ID to other devices. Z-Wave controllers can exist in different shapes:

- as a remote control,
- as PC software in conjunction with a Z-Wave transceiver connected in the PC (typically via USB),
- as a gateway or as
- a wall switch with special controller function.

> Important: A Z-Wave controller is a controller because it can assign his own Home-ID to other devices and also assigns an individual Node-IDs. Slaves are Z-Wave devices that cannot assign their own Home-ID nor can they assign Node-IDs.

The Home-ID of a controller cannot be changed by the user [2] and becomes the common Home-ID of all devices, which were included by this controller.

The controller that begins to build up a network is transferring its Home-ID to other devices and becomes the designated **Primary Controller** of this network. In a bigger network, several controllers can work together, but there is always only one controller with the privilege to assign IDs - the primary controller. All other controllers are called **Secondary controllers**.

The primary controller includes other nodes into the network by assigning them its own Home-ID. If a node accepts the Home-ID of the primary controller, this node becomes part of the network. Besides assigning the Home-ID, the primary controller also assigns an individual Node-ID to the new included device. This process is referred to as **Inclusion**.

Note: The definition and the process to use Home-ID and Node-ID is part of the ITU-T G.9959. However, the process of assign-

---

[2]A factory reset of a Z-Wave controller generates a new randomly picked Home-ID.

	Definition	In the Controller	In the Slave
Home-ID	The Home-ID is the common identification of a Z-Wave network	The Home-ID is already available at factory default.	No Home-ID at factory default
Node-ID	The Node-ID is the individual identification (address) of a node within a common network	Controller has its own Node-ID predefined (typically 0x01)	Is assigned by the primary controller

Table 3.3: Home-ID and Node-ID

ing a Home-ID and Node-ID—the inclusion process–remains the intellectual property of Silicon Labs (for more information about the legal situation of Z-Wave, please refer to Chapter 6.1).

In Figure 3.5, four devices are available in factory-default state. There are two controllers with a preset Home-ID. Two other devices cannot operate as a controller (slave) and, hence, have no Home-ID of their own.

Depending on which of the controllers is used to build up a Z-Wave network, the network Home-ID in this example will be either 0x00001111 or 0x00002222.

Both controllers have the same Node-ID 1. The slave devices do not have any Node-ID assigned. In theory, this picture shows two networks with one node in each of them. Because none of the nodes in the figure has any common Home-ID, no communication can take place.

One of the two controllers is now selected as being the primary controller of the network. This controller assigns his Home-ID

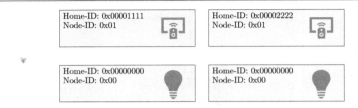

Figure 3.5: Z-Wave devices before inclusion in a network

to all the other devices (in Z-Wave terms is "includes them") and also assigns their individual Node-ID. The second controller assumes the same Home-ID as the inclusion or primary controller. After successful inclusion, all nodes have the same Home-ID, i.e. they are connected in one network with each other. At the same time, every node has a different individual Node-ID. Only with this individual Node-IDs, can they be distinguished from each other and can communicate with each other. **In a Z-Wave network nodes having a common Home-ID must ever have the same Node-ID**.

In the network shown as an example in Figure 3.6, there are two controllers. The controller whose Home-ID became the Home-ID of all devices is the primary controller. All other controllers become secondary controllers.

A secondary controller is also a controller from the technical point of view and does not differ from the primary controller. However, only the controller with the privilege being the primary controller can include further devices. (If an SIS is present, every controller can include device by executing the Node-ID assignment done by the SIS. For more information about SIS, please refer to Chapter 3.5.1).

Because the nodes of different networks cannot communicate with each other due to different Home-IDs, they can coexist and do not even "see" each other. This is shown in Figure 3.7.

The 32-bit long Home-ID allows distinguishing up to 4 billion

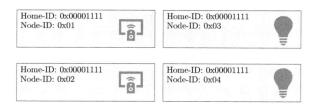

Figure 3.6: Network after successful Inclusion

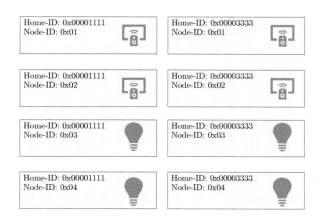

Figure 3.7: Two Z-Wave-Networks with different Home-IDs co-exist

(2^{32}) different Z-Wave networks with a maximum number of $2^8 = 256$ different nodes.

It is not possible for one single node to have two different Home-IDs or Node-IDs. There are devices (the so-called bridge controllers) that allow bridging two different networks but they consist of two independent Z-Wave nodes with an interconnection at a higher layer. Within their individual Z-Wave networks they still appear as a simple node.

3.1.4   Network Transport Function

After looking at the way the networks are identified and the nodes are identified within the network, we now need to look how data is sent over the air. This is managed by the next layer in the layered communications stack, the Network Transport Layer.

The transport function uses up to 64 bytes of the PHY/MAC frame to transport network relevant data plus the application data itself. The allocation of these bytes is again defined as a frame, now the transport frame.

Figure 3.8 shows the definition of the Transport frame according to the specification ITU-T G.9959 resp. Z-Wave.

All Z-Wave data packets in the network are identified by their Home-IDs and the Node- IDs of sender and receiver. The other data elements are used to either manage the packet itself (length, checksum) or to control the flow of packets in the network. This task is accomplished by the frame control bytes. They have the structure shown in Table 3.4.

Besides the obvious and straightforward communication pattern where one transmitter sends data to one receiver, technically referred to as *Singlecast*, there are other possible patterns of communication in a wireless network.

Singlecast   A packet is sent from a transmitter to a receiver.

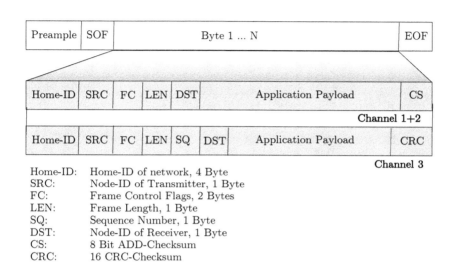

Home-ID: Home-ID of network, 4 Byte
SRC: Node-ID of Transmitter, 1 Byte
FC: Frame Control Flags, 2 Bytes
LEN: Frame Length, 1 Byte
SQ: Sequence Number, 1 Byte
DST: Node-ID of Receiver, 1 Byte
CS: 8 Bit ADD-Checksum
CRC: 16 CRC-Checksum

Figure 3.8: Transport Frame Layout for Singlecast

Byte	Bit	Function
1	0...3	Header type
1	4	Speed
1	5	Low power flag
1	6	Ack / Req
1	7	Routed
2	0...3	Sequence number
2	5...	Beam Control

Table 3.4: Bit Assignment of MAC Frame

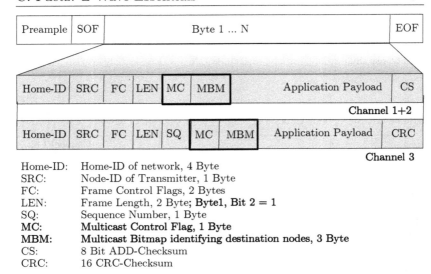

Figure 3.9: Transport Frame Layout for Multicast

Broadcast   All packets sent to the Node-ID ($255 = \texttt{0xff}$) are considered as broadcast. This means they are received by all nodes in the network. The frame format of a broadcast frame does not differ from the frame format of a single cast or point-to-point frame.

Multicast   In a multicast communication, one sender sends a data packet to multiple recipients. While this is always achievable by sending multiple identical singlecast packets to a list of destinations, the multicast operation simplifies and accelerates such a function. There are two ways to encode multiple addresses in one transport frame:

- Each address of the receiving devices is listed in the frame, one after each other.
- There is a bitmask where each receiver is represented by one single bit. If this bit is set to '1' the corresponding

Node is supposed to receive the packet.

The first approach takes less space in the frame if there are only few receivers of a multicast message. The second approach always takes a fixed amount of space regardless of the number of receivers.

Z-Wave used the second approach and allocates 29 Byte (232 possible devices divided by 8 bit per Byte) in the multicast frame as shown in figure 3.9.

This means that different communication patterns offer different amounts of data that can be transported in a Z-Wave transport frame.

- Singlecast: 54 Byte
- Multicast: 26 Byte
- Broadcast: 54 Byte

3.1.5 Data Reliability and Error Correction

In order to verify that the data packet was received correctly, an 8-bit checksum byte is added to the data frame in communication Channels 1 and 2. This checksum covers the whole frame and a frame is only considered a valid frame if this checksum is detected as correct.

The checksum is calculated in a simple way. It is just combining all bytes of the frame (from Home-ID to the last byte prior to the checksum itself) using an exclusive OR. In the programming language C, this algorithm can be describes as:

Listing 3.1: Z-Wave Check Sum in C

```c
Byte GenerateCheckSum (Byte *Data, Byte Length)
{
        Byte checksum = 0xff;
        for (; Length > 0; Length --)
                checksum ^= *Data++;
        return checksum;
}
```

This simple checksum algorithm and the fact that this single byte needs to protect up to 63 bytes of data is a clear weakness of Z-Wave as for almost all other wireless protocols that were designed for home control. Stronger protection of data was thus introduced later on as a feature of the application layer (see Chapter 5.4.7). A simple example will illustrate this fact:

> Let us assume a data stream of the two bytes 0x01 and 0x80 (the first byte has only the least significant byte as 1, all others are 0, the next byte only has the most significant byte as 1, the others are zero).
>
> The Z-Wave checksum algorithm will use the start value of 0xff, run two iterations, and generate a checksum byte of 0b01111110 or 0x7f. In case the two bytes of the data stream are just twisted to 0x01, 0x80, the very same checksum algorithm will generate the very same checksum of 0b01111110 or 0x7f.
>
> This shows that such a weak algorithm can hardly detect small changes in the data packet. The checksum has only $1 : 2^8$ or $1 : 256$ different values, hence the chance that a random data stream is wrongly detected as valid frame is also $1 : 2^8$ or $1 : 256$.
>
> The situation in Z-Wave is less critical because a frame will only be accepted by the receiver if
>
> - the checksum is correct **and**
> - the Home-ID of 4 Byte is matching the Home-ID of the receiving device **and**
> - the Node-ID of 1 Byte is matching the Node-ID of the receiving device.
>
> This results in a chance of $1 : 2^{42}$ that a random byte stream will be accepted as valid frame and used for the application.

In communication Channel 3, a CRC-16 checksum is used. The CRC-16 generator polynomial is:

$P(x) = x16+x12+x5+1$, also known as CRC–CCITT

The CRC 16 is calculated over the whole frame, except for the preamble, SOF, and the CRC-16 field itself. The CRC-16 generator is initialized to 0x1D0F before applying the first frame byte of a frame and no bits are appended to the frame data. CRC 16 does show the weaknesses of the 8 bit checksum.

3.1.6 Acknowledged Communication

In many wireless communication networks, a communication between a sender and a receiver is accomplished by simply sending a message over the air from the source to the destination. In case this message gets lost (due to interference or distant positioning of the receiver from the sender), the sender does not get any feedback if the message was received and the receiver was able to execute the command properly. This may result in stability problems and frustrate the user of such a network. In Z-Wave the receiver has to acknowledge every command sent by the transmitter. This gives an indication whether the communication was successful or not.

> A communication in Z-Wave was successful if the sending data packet (1) was received with correct checksum (2) and correct Home-ID (3) and correct Node-ID by the receiver AND the sender (4) has received an acknowledgement packet - again (5) with correct checksum and (6) correct Home-ID and (7) correct Node-ID - from the destination.

The process can be illustrated by comparing it with the traditional postal mail service.

Not having acknowledged messages is like sending a normal standard letter to a destination. In most of the cases, this letter will

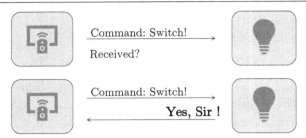

Figure 3.10: Communication with and without acknowledgement

be delivered correctly and the receiver will be able to read the letter. However, there is no guarantee and some uncertainty remains.

Important messages are therefore to send as **registered letter with return receipt**. Here the sender has a written proof that his letter was delivered correctly and handed over to the receiver.

Even a **registered letter with return receipt** does not guarantee that the letter will always be delivered correctly. However, the sender will get an indication when a receiver has for instance moved out of town and can do other actions to make sure the letter will finally reach its destination.

In Z-Wave, the return receipt is called **Acknowledge (ACK)**. If no ACK is received, the transmitter waits for random time between 20 ms and 100 ms and retry two more times. After three unsuccessful attempts, the Z-Wave transceiver gives up and reports a failure. Z-Wave devices then look for an alternative way to deliver the packet. This is called routing and will be described in Chapter 3.2.

The number of unsuccessful transmission attempts can indicate the quality of wireless connection. The communication with and without acknowledgement is shown in Figure 3.10. The only exception to this process are broadcast messages and multicast messages. They are not confirmed.

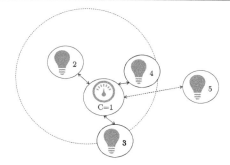

Figure 3.11: Network without routing

3.2   Routing

3.2.1   Routing Basics

In a simple wireless communication network, all devices can communicate directly over the air; they are called **in wireless range** or short **in range**. This means that they are close enough to each other to "see" each other with their "wireless eyes." If a node— for whatever reason—drops out of the wireless range, it is no longer reachable and all communication of this node and to this node will fail.

Figure 3.11 shows such a simple network. From the controller (Node-ID = 1) point of view nodes 2, 3 and 4 are reachable. Node 5 however is not existent for the controller since it's not in direct range.

In case there is no successful communication to this node 5 from the controller, this node will now be considered as non-existing or gone.

If a communications network is not even using a wireless acknowledgement, the controller will not even realize that his communication partner will never get his messages. The sender will still assume proper execution of the commands sent. This is certainly

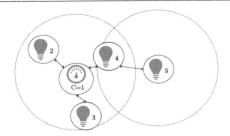

Figure 3.12: Z-Wave network with routing

not an acceptable function of a wireless communication network
and would not be considered as "reliable communication."

Z-Wave is a wireless system that offers a very powerful mechanism to overcome this limitation. Besides the confirmation of
every packet sent—introduced in Chapter 3.1.5— Z-Wave nodes
can also forward and repeat messages on behalf of other devices
if these devices are not in a direct range to each other. This has
two remarkable advantages:

- It extends the wireless range of the network because messages can reach their destination via multiple hops.
- If a communication fails, there may be a backup option—a
  plan B. The sender can just ask other nodes to help out
  and choose a different route to its desired destination.

Figure 3.12 shows the same network again with the controller as
Node-ID 1 communicating directly to the nodes 2, 3 and 4. Node
5 lies outside of its radio range but it is within the radio range
of node 4. Therefore, the controller can communicate to node 5
via node 4. The wireless way from node 1 via node 4 to node 5
is called **a route**.

A network that has various ways to communicate between different nodes using other nodes as routers is called a **meshed
network**.

Z-Wave can route messages via up to four repeating nodes. This

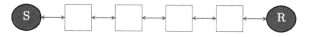

Figure 3.13: Maximum route between 2 nodes via 4 repeaters

is a compromise between the network size, robustness, and the maximum time a message is allowed to travel in the network. The maximum route between two nodes via four repeaters is shown in Figure 3.13.

Assuming, the maximum radio range with a good antenna and low noise floor is up to 200 meters. Routing could in theory extend the wireless coverage of a Z-Wave network to almost 1 kilometer. This is certainly a corner case far from reality. However, it is good to know that a Z-Wave network with its two functions 'confirmation or acknowledgement of messages' and 'routing of messages' is more than able to establish a robust network within even larger residential homes or offices.

Long routes are possible but not desirable. Let's apply some math again:

Table 3.2 has shown that a single frame of minimal size may still take about 20 ms to be transmitted. The same time is needed to transmit the returning ACK-command. Since the routers need to fully receive the whole packet before it can be resent again (store-and-forward), the travel time over a route of full length will be 5 * 2 * 20 ms = 200 ms.

In case there are more packets to be exchanged to execute a single function on the receiving node, the delay caused by communication can reach a level that is perceived as too slow by the user.

Nevertheless, even if the network consists only of nodes in direct range, it is good to know that the network has plenty of fall back options, just in case.

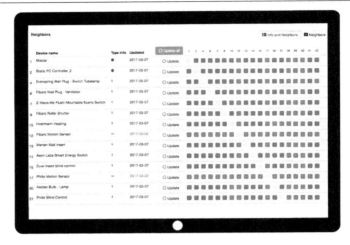

Figure 3.14: Some controller show their 'routing table' keys granted (Source: Certified Installer Toolkit)

3.2.2   The Routing Algorithm

The primary controller of a network is responsible for building and maintaining the knowledge about routes in the network. Every node is able to determine which nodes are in direct wireless range. These nodes are called **neighbors**. During inclusion and the later request by the primary controller, the nodes can inform the primary controller about their actual neighbor nodes. Using this information, the controller is able to build a table that has all the information about possible communication routes in the network. This table is called **routing table**, but it does not contain the routes but the neighborhood situation of the network. Some controllers display this table in their user interface, as shown in Figure 3.14.

The controller uses the information in this table to determine the shortest and most reliable route between two communication partners. Once determined the route remains valid until

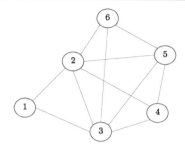

Figure 3.15: Example of a meshed network

	to 1	to 2	to 3	to 4	to 5	to 6
Send to node 1						
Send to node 2						
Send to node 3						
Send to node 4						
Send to node 5						
Send to node 6						

Black: no direct wireless range
Grey: in direct wireless range

Figure 3.16: Routing Table for Example network

some communication on this route fails. Each packet, which is supposed to be sent using other nodes, has the full information about the desired route in the packet header. It is not possible to change this route on the fly during the way of the packet in the network.

Figure 3.15 shows an example of a meshed network with one controller and five other nodes. The controller as primary controller has Node-ID 1. It can communicate directly with nodes 2 and 3. There is no direct connection between node 1 and nodes 4, 5, 6. A neighborhood table for the example network is presented in Figure 3.16.

The routing algorithm inside the controller tries to find the short-

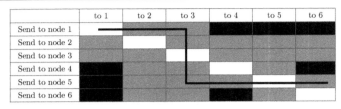

	to 1	to 2	to 3	to 4	to 5	to 6
Send to node 1						
Send to node 2						
Send to node 3						
Send to node 4						
Send to node 5						
Send to node 6						

Black: no direct wireless range
Grey: in direct wireless range

Figure 3.17: Routing from Node 1 via Node 3 to Node 6

Figure 3.18: Multiple communication attempts in Z-Wave - step 1

est route to the destination. In case of the example used here, there are two equally good alternatives:

- $1 \rightarrow 3 \rightarrow 4$ or
- $1 \rightarrow 2 \rightarrow 4$.

Figure 3.17 explains how the route fits into the routing table. There are there alternatives too.

The routing decision is made prior to sending the packet and the full route is encoded into the packet itself. This approach is called **static source routing** and it is the best way to execute routing in a low energy network such as Z-Wave because it avoids rerouting attempts within the networks. Nevertheless, the transmitter itself is still generating overhead traffic if a routing attempt fails.

Figure 3.18 to 3.20 shows such a rerouting attempt with its consequences. In the first figure the direct communication between the transmitter 'S' and the receiver 'R' fails. None of the three

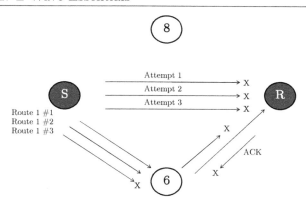

Figure 3.19: Multiple communication attempts in Z-Wave - step 2

packets reaches the receiver and is confirmed. (It is irrelevant if the packet itself fails or the acknowledgement packet. In both cases the transmitter does not have the assurance that his command was received.)

As a next step, the transmitter tries an alternative route, in case of this example he is using Node 6 as a router.

This scenario shows different cases in which a communication can fail. The first communication attempt fails between node 6 and the destination. The second attempt even reaches the receiver, but the acknowledgment packet gets lost. The third attempt does not even reach the routing node.

The sender will try three times on three different routes to reach the receiver. Figure 3.20 illustrates the finally successful attempt using node 8 as router.

In case the third routing attempt fails the transmitter will stop further communication and report back an error. He will however remember the failed routes and tries even different - and likely longer routes in the next attempt.

In case the algorithm finds a new route, this route is cached and

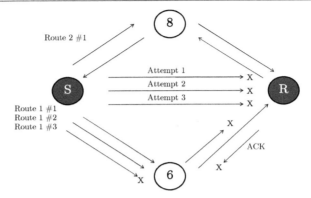

Figure 3.20: Multiple communication attempts in Z-Wave - step 3

used in future communication.

The three figures 3.18 to 3.20 illustrate the escalation strategy of the routing algorithms. It's also obvious that particularly with longer routes the number of packets of an rerouting attempt may reach large numbers and easily exceed 100 packets.

Therefore, the worst case is a situation where routes permanently change and rerouting is needed often. This may happen when, for example, a metal fire protection door is sometimes open and sometimes closed and reflects wireless signals.

Since the routing information must be carried within the transport frame, the amount of space available for payload data is reduced by 5 Bytes. Figure 3.21 shows how the frame type changes when routing information is added.

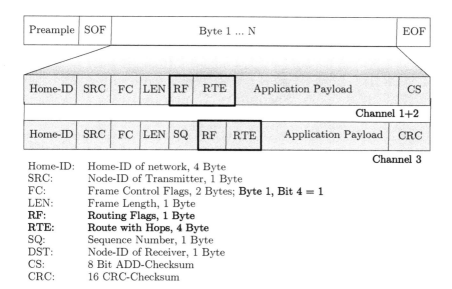

Home-ID: Home-ID of network, 4 Byte
SRC: Node-ID of Transmitter, 1 Byte
FC: Frame Control Flags, 2 Bytes; **Byte 1, Bit 4 = 1**
LEN: Frame Length, 1 Byte
RF: **Routing Flags, 1 Byte**
RTE: **Route with Hops, 4 Byte**
SQ: Sequence Number, 1 Byte
DST: Node-ID of Receiver, 1 Byte
CS: 8 Bit ADD-Checksum
CRC: 16 CRC-Checksum

Figure 3.21: Routing Information changes the Transport Frame

3.3   Device and Network Types

3.3.1   Role in Network: Controller and Slaves

The previous chapter already mentioned the existence of two different device types:

- Controllers and
- Slaves.

The most obvious difference between a controller and a slave is the ability to build and manage a network. This is only possible with a controller. The controller that is used to include new nodes into the network by assigning its Home-ID and providing a Node-ID is referred to as the **Primary Controller**. All other controllers are called **Secondary Controllers**. Controllers are further differentiated according to their mobility.

- Portable Controllers are battery operated and can be moved around.
- Static Controllers are mains powered and they are installed on a fixed location.

Another differentiation between node types comes from the way a node handles routing information resp. stores information about the structure of the network. The knowledge about the network and the different routes to other nodes determines the communication abilities of a given controller and slaves. Here Z-Wave distinguishes between normal slaves and routing slaves. Normal slaves do not know any routes to communication partners and can therefore only answer to requests where the route of the incoming packet is copied for the acknowledgement and answer. *Routing slaves* [3] on the other hand know some preset routes and can therefore initiate a communication by themselves.

---

[3]Routing Slave is a misleading term because it suggests that this device is routing messages. All Z-Wave devices that are mains powered can and will route messages. The specific function of the routing slave is the ability to store several routes to destinations and therefore the ability to send unsolicited messages.

Table 3.5 shows the different node types with their knowledge about the network and subsequently their communication abilities:

This comparison gives rise to a number of basic rules:

- Every Z-Wave device can receive and acknowledge messages.
- Controllers can send messages to all nodes in the network, solicited and unsolicited (*The master can talk whenever he wants and to whom he wants.*).
- Slaves cannot send unsolicited messages but only answer to requests (*The slave shall only speak up when he is asked.*).
- Routing slaves can answer requests and they are allowed to send unsolicited messages to certain nodes the controller has predefined (*The sender slave is still a slave but - on permission - he may speak up.*).

Since the functionality of standard slaves is quite limited, this type of node is only used for fixed location mains powered devices such as dimmers or switches. Every kind of sensor or any device that can be used on multiple locations must be a routing slave or even a controller because he may be required to send out certain information unsolicited. Meanwhile, only few legacy devices are still operating as standard slaves while all devices that entered the market after 2008 have routing capabilities.

Typical applications of slaves are shown in Table 3.6.

3.3.2   Different ways to power devices

The way a node is powered significantly determines its ability to communicate. A node that has plenty of energy can stay awake with its receiver turned on and immediately react on all messages sent to this node. In case where a node is powered by a battery or even with energy harvesting technology energy saving is critical. Such a device needs to be in deep sleep state or even turned off most of the time and can therefore not easily be reached by other

	Neighbors	Route	Possible functions
Controller	Knows all neighbors	Has access to the complete routing table	Can communicate with every device in the network, if a route exists.
Slave	Knows all neighbors	Has no information about the routing table	Can only reply to the node that he has received the message from. Hence, can not send unsolicited messages
Routing Slave	Knows all neighbors	Has partial knowledge about the routing table	Can reply to the node that he has received the message from and can send unsolicited messages to a number of predefined nodes he has a route to.

Table 3.5: Properties of the Z-Wave device models

Device Type	Application
Slave	Only fixed installed mains powered devices like wall switches, wall dimmers or Venetian blind controllers
Routing Slave	Battery-operated devices and mobile applicable devices such as sensors with battery operation, wall plugs for Schuko and plug types, thermostats and heaters with battery operation, and all other slave applications, as well as all new devices including fixed installation wall devices, are routing slaves.

Table 3.6: Typical applications for slaves

Figure 3.22: CO2 sensor, mains powered (Source: SIEGENIA-AUBI KG)

nodes.

Mains Powered Devices

Mains powered devices are always in reception mode and can receive and acknowledge wireless messages. The same time they can act as routers for other devices. All devices, that handle mains power (switches, dimmers, blind controls) are typically mains powered because they are connected to the mains power signals anyway. Other devices need an additional connection to the mains, either as a built-in power supply or as an external power brick. A typical reason is a high-power consumption caused by the main function of the device or the desire to be independent of any battery.

Figure 3.22 shows as an example a CO2-sensor that is mains powered because the CO2-sensor component needs too much power.

> Important: Only mains powered devices can act as Z-Wave routers.

A very important mains-powered device is the static controller. This is a controller that is always wirelessly active and can therefore fulfill certain management roles within the Z-Wave network. Additionally, the static controller typically serves the graphical user interface.

Battery-Operated Devices

The main objective of a battery-operated device is to preserve the battery power and only use as much battery power as needed. Battery-powered devices are therefore in a deep-sleep state most of the time only consuming minimal amount of power. In deep-sleep state they are not able to communicate with other devices.

In order to communicate with other devices, the battery-operated device needs to be woken up and sent to deep sleep mode right after communication takes place. To maintain a minimal level of responsiveness, to provide for configuration messages from time to time, and to use battery-operated devices, Z-Wave offers three basic solutions:

1. Devices with manual wakeup
2. Devices with wakeup intervals
3. Frequently listening battery devices

Energy Harvesting

A lot of devices cannot be mains powered, but the increasing need for batteries requires effort and generates a lot of waste. An elegant solution to this problem is **Energy Harvesting**. This technology attempts to generate energy from the environment. Typical sources of energy are:

- Solar: Solar cells directly convert solar energy into electrical energy.
- Wind: Turbines harvest this energy and generate electrical energy.
- Temperature Differences: So-called "Peltier" elements can

Figure 3.23: Z-Weather, the first Z-Wave device based on energy harvesting (Source: www.popp.eu)

generate electrical energy out of minimal temperature differences of few Kelvin.

- Vibration or movements: Electromechanical converters are used to generate electrical energy.
- Mechanical Pressure: Piezo-elements are able to generate energy.

The beauty of devices powered by energy harvesting is that they do not need any maintenance anymore. The challenge of this approach is the very little energy the harvesters are able to generate. The wireless technology EnOcean (see Chapter 1.5 for details) was developed in the late 1990s with special focus on energy harvesting. The results are devices that run completely battery-free, but at the same time the defined wireless protocol misses important functions such as sufficient security. The very small packets that EnOcean uses to preserve energy do not allow more complex operations such as firmware update and the protocol will not route and cannot reconfirm messages.
[4]

---

[4]Meanwhile EnOcean also offers a two-way communication with Acknowledgement, but these devices require a battery.

The Z-Wave protocol was not developed with a focus on super-low energy consumption. Using energy harvesting is therefore a challenge. Using the Series 500 IC set, only one single supplier was able so far to develop Z-Wave products using energy harvesting. The Popp Z-Weather shown in Figure 3.23 was the very first battery-free Z-Wave device powered by a small solar panel only. To achieve this ambitious goal, few optimizations were needed:

- The device stores energy in an internal very large capacitor to survive the night time.
- The device need to see the sun every day, however it will cope with short days and cloudy weather conditions during winter time.
- The device distinguished between essential functions and not essential functions. Essential is the emergency message in case of heavy wind. To make sure there is always enough energy available other non-essential functions such as temperature or humidity reporting may be delayed in case the energy budget does not allow more frequent reporting.
- The device has one more internal very energy efficient microcontroller managing the energy budget. The more energy hungry Z-Wave IC will only be fired up when really needed.

The new Series 700 Z-Wave ASICs from Silicon Labs are focused on the lower energy consumption to enable energy-harvesting applications using Z-Wave. It can be expected that more Z-Wave devices will use energy harvesting in the near future.

From the network point of view, energy-harvesting devices will act like other battery-operated devices.

Manual Wakeup

In case a device is only required to send out information, when it is used it can remain in deep sleep most of the time. A good example of such a device is a remote control. Once configured, the remote is only operating when in users hand and a button is pressed. At this precise moment, the device needs to wake up and send out a wireless signal, but it can go back to deep sleep state right afterwards.

This very simple and efficient way to save battery life comes at a price. A central controller in a Z-Wave network cannot track whether or not the remote control or any other device with manual wakeup still exists. There is no heartbeat or any other regular event that would inform the rest of the network about status of the device.

During inclusion and at every change of configuration, the user needs to make sure the device is manually woken up and was able to receive the messages. Sometimes a simple click of a button handles this job. However, some devices require special sequences to activate a wakeup that allows the device to communicate with the controller that is configuring the device. The message sent to this controller informing about the wakeup state is called **wakeup notification**.

Figure 3.24 shows a remote control that requires a special key sequence to wake up and inform the controller about the wakeup status.

Devices with wakeup interval

Devices with a fixed wakeup interval also remain in deep sleep state most of the time. A built-in clock will wake up the device regularly. The device will indicate its awakening by sending out a **wakeup notification** to the controller that manages the device and queues the messages. Typical wakeup intervals are between few minutes and several days. Chapter 4.2.5 describes the process in detail and gives some battery lifetime estimations.

The advantage of the wakeup interval is that the device regularly issues a kind of heartbeat. This allows the controller to determine the health status of the device and issue an alert message to

Figure 3.24: Remote Control as example for a battery device with manual wakeup (Source: www.z-wave.me)

the user if a battery-operated device did not wake up for a long period. This could be due to a dead battery, but it is also possible that the device was removed or damaged. In case the controller wants to change some configurations, these messages will eventually reach the device without further manual interaction. Of course, it is always possible to manually wake up a device with wakeup interval, e.g. to speed up configuration changes.

A frequent status message is particularly important for devices that can cause major damage when not functioning. Figure 3.25 shows some sensors as an example for devices with wakeup interval.

Typical applications for devices with wakeup interval are sensors.

Frequent wakeup - the FLiRS concept

Actuators like door locks or sirens need to react to wireless commands right away. Nevertheless, there may be good reasons to operate them by battery. It gives more flexibility for installation and certain devices can't be mains powered because they are mounted on moving parts.

Figure 3.25: Sensor as an example of a device with wakeup interval (Source: Fibaro Group)

The trick to implement battery operated actuators is called **FLiRS (Frequently Listening Routing Slaves)**.

A FLiRS device is still battery operated and needs to stay in deep sleep mode most of the time. However, the FLiRS device wakes up every 250 ms or every second and checks if there is a signal on its operating frequency. This test can be done very fast and does not need any further wireless communication. In case there is no signal on the frequency, the device will go back into deep sleep right away. If a signal is received, the device will remain awake and try to decode a Z-Wave frame (for more information about the Z-Wave frame, refer to Chapter 3.1.2).

In order to communicate with such a FLiRS device the transceiver needs to send a so-called **Wakeup Beam**. This is a permanent wireless signal that is slightly longer than the wakeup interval of the FLiRS device (250 or 1000 ms). This ensures that there is a wireless signal on the frequency when the FLiRS devices wakes up.

Figure 3.26 shows the process with the wakeup beam, the awakening of the FLiRS and the subsequent exchange of information.

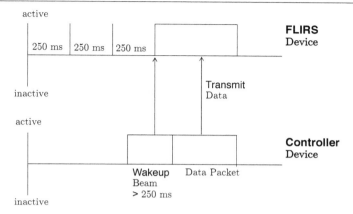

Figure 3.26: Wakeup-Beam wakes up a FLiRS device

Chapter 4.2.5 gives some further information about the battery consumption of a FLiRS device. It is a compromise between the need for wireless control and the lowest battery consumption possible. Typical FLiRS devices are all battery operated actuators such as door locks or sirens. Figure 3.27 shows an example of an alarm siren that can be mounted on different places without need for mains power.

Although FLiRS devices can be woken up from a transmitter, they are **not used** for routing in a Z-Wave network to preserve battery power.

3.3.3 Summary

Table 3.7 shows what kind of Z-Wave node type combinations are possible.

Z-Wave Plus has introduced the Network Role Type, further formalizing the possible combinations of controller, slave, and powering options. A Z-Wave Plus device must follow one of the following Network Role Type models:

Figure 3.27: Siren as FLiRS device (Source: www.popp.eu)

Device Type	Controller	Routing Slave	Slave
Mains	yes, called static controller	yes	yes
Battery with wakeup interval	unlikely	yes	no
Battery with FLiRS	unlikely	yes	possible but rare
Manual wakeup	yes, portable controllers	possible but rare	no

Table 3.7: Possible combinations of node types

- **Central Static Controller (CSC)**: This is the central gateway, a mains powered static controller possessing the primary controller role. The CSC must provide routing for other nodes.

- **Sub Static Controller (SSC)**: This is a static controller not capable of providing SUC and SIS functions. SSCs must provide routing for other nodes.

- **Portable Controller (PC)**: This is the normal remote control. Such a device will not be visible to the CSC since its never reporting any value except when using. PCs do not provide routing for other nodes.

- **Portable Reporting Controller (PRC)**: This is a remote control that is capable to report status information to the central controller. PRCs do not provide routing for other nodes.

- **Portable Slave (PS)**: If a device is battery operated and can move but will not be moved all the time, e.g. a battery-operated scene controller—this role type can be used. PSs do not provide routing for other nodes.

- **Always On Slave (AOS)**: Actuators like switches, dimmers, motor controls are mains powered. AOS must provide routing for other nodes.

- **Sleeping Reporting Slave (SRS)**: This is the role type for all almost all digital or analog battery operated sensors. SRSs do not provide routing for other nodes.

- **Reachable Sleeping Slave (RSS)**: This is the role type for FLiRS devices. RSSs do not provide routing for other nodes.

3.4 Manual Update of the network

3.4.1 Exclusion - Removal of functioning devices

The exclusion of a device is reverting the actions performed for inclusion. The Home-ID of the network is deleted in the device and all information of this device is deleted from the routing tables of the network as well.

The normal way to exclude a device is to perform an **exclusion process**. In most cases, this is similar to the inclusion process. The excluded device needs to confirm the exclusion. This means the device to be excluded needs to be present in the network and need to have a wireless connection to the primary controller. The primary controller will send an exclusion request to the device and this device needs to agree to the exclusion by confirming that the old Home-ID was successfully deleted. There is a manual interaction needed on the device to confirm the exclusion. This confirmation of the device is needed for the primary controller to update its routing table.

Security Aspects on inclusion and exclusion Inclusion and Exclusion operations require a manual action on the device so physical access to the device is required. A controller needs to send out an information that it will include/exclude and the device itself will answer depending on the manual interaction, typically pushing a button. This will ensure that only devices that are in physical possession of the owner can be excluded or included.

To further increase convenience in Z-Wave some devices support the so-called **auto-inclusion**.

In this case the manual interaction to confirm inclusion is replaced by the operation initially powering the device. Devices with auto inclusion function will accept any inclusion attempt from a controller within a certain time - typically 30 seconds - after initial power on. Essentially the auto inclusion combines the necessary process of powering with the also necessary process of inclusion into one single step.

This simplifies the building of Z-Wave networks, but this also implies a risk that a different controller is first asking the fresh and new device to be included.

However, the legal owner of the device has always the chance to exclude the device from the network since he is in physical possession of the device. Exclusion can therefore be done again

- from any controller issuing an exclusion request,
- if and only if there is a manual confirmation on the device.

For more information about security and authentication please refer to chapter 4.5.

3.4.2 Removal of defective devices - Failed Node List

The routing table in the primary controller always shows the actual status of all devices in the network after inclusion of the latest device. During normal operation, a node can

- go out of operation (damaged) or
- can be moved to a different location.

In both cases, the routing table is no longer valid and communication to the moved or damaged node may fail (if the node is just moved, it is possible that it was moved luckily in direct range of the controller or into a place where his old neighbors can still reach him).

Any failed communication to a node causes an error. Consequently, the controller will mark this node as failed node by putting him into a so-called **failed node list**. The failed node list contains nodes with failed communication. Being in the failed node list does not necessarily mean that the node is permanently gone. Any working communication will move the node back into the original routing table.

If no successful communication happens, the node will stay in the

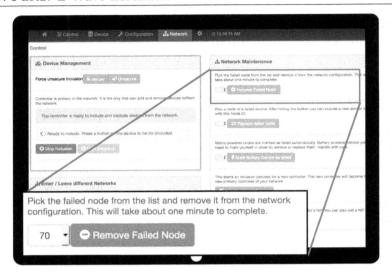

Figure 3.28: Screenshot of a Z-Wave Controller with a button to exclude a failed node (Source: Certified Installer Toolkit)

failed node list and can be removed from the network without any cooperation of the failed node.

The reason for this is obvious. Failed nodes can no longer communicate their agreement to the exclusion.

In order to force a node out of the network, certain requirements need to be made:

1. The node needs to be in the failed node list.
2. The controller needs to receive a command from the user to force the node out of the network. The controller will never automatically perform such an action.
3. After the command to force out a node the controller will do a very last attempt to reach this node and will only execute the exclusion if this last attempt fails as well.

Figure 3.28 shows a user dialog to enable removing a failed node from the network.

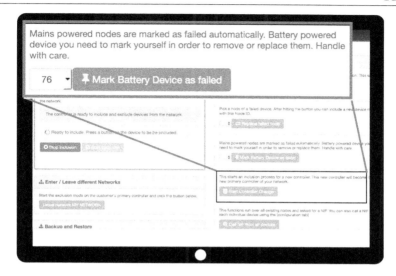

Figure 3.29: Screenshot of a Z-Wave Controller that allows to mark nodes as failed (Source: Certified Installer Toolkit)

Battery-operated devices with wakeup interval or manual wakeup will never enter into the failed node list, since the controller knows that it is not possible to just send them messages. Since there are plenty of reasons why these battery-operated devices may not announce their wakeup to the controller—e.g. no button is pressed on a remote control for some time—the controller cannot just assume they are gone.

The main function of the failed node list is to exclude devices from further routing attempts. Since battery-operated devices do not route at all, there is no pressing need to remove them from the network. Some Z-Wave controllers, however, allow moving battery-operated devices manually into the failed node list in order to exclude them in a second step—just for cosmetic reasons—Figure 3.29 shows an example of such a user dialog.

3.4.3 Network Reorganization

The process to update the controller(s) about the new status of the network including all routing information in all devices is called network reorganization. Some controller interfaces may also call it **network redetection** or **network repair**.

In all cases, the following functions are performed:

1. The primary controller will ask all known nodes to rediscover their neighbors and to report an updated list of neighbors back to the controller.

2. Depending on the implementation the controller may inform all other controllers about the new status and update their routing tables as well.

3. Depending on the implementation the controller will also update all routing slaves about changed routes.

Depending on the size of the network this rediscovery process may take some time and create a lot of network traffic. This operation will therefore not be executed automatically by the controller but on user request only. Certain controllers allow setting up a periodic network rediscovery, typically at nighttime, when the high traffic does not interfere with user interactions. A special challenge comes from battery-operated devices that may need to be updated. The controller will have to wait for the next wakeup of these devices and in case of portable controllers that only wake up when manually operated, this may take a long time. Figure 3.30 shows a web browser interface for a network reorganisation.

3.5 Automated Updating of the network

Besides manual processes to change the network configuration, Z-Wave offers several ways to automatically update the network and fix problems behind the scene. It is certainly not possible to repair damaged devices, but the aim of these processes is to

Figure 3.30: Screenshot of Webbrowser Interface for Network Reorganisation (Source: Expert User Interface of Z-Way by z-wave.me)

fix routing problems and to make sure a transmitter can find a receiver as long as there is a receiver.

Z-Wave uses two different approaches to ensure this:

1. The **Static Update-Controller** is a special function of a static controller to synchronize routing tables of the different controllers and routing slaves of the network.

2. **Explorer Frames** are special transport frames that do not contain routing information but have a built in mechanism to find their way within the network.

The first mechanism introduced into the Z-Wave protocol was the static update controller. Later, the Explorer Frame technology was added.

3.5.1 Static Update Controller

Static controllers are Z-Wave controllers that are mains powered and thus permanently wirelessly active and available for other devices to communicate with. This is the basis to act in two special functions a controller can have—Static Update Controller and Static ID Server. Both functions are available one time only in a network, and in most cases, they are performed by one single controller. In case there are more than one static controller in the network, they have to negotiate who is performing the function. This happens automatically without any interaction or influence by the user.

Static Update-Controller (SUC)

The Static Update Controller (SUC) is a special function of a static controller. Every static controller (a controller with fixed location and powered by mains power) must be able to perform as a SUC. Sometimes the function typically needs to be activated first but most modern controllers will automatically seek to become SUC. **The SUC acts as a known central entity** that always has the latest and therefore most valid routing table of the network. For all other devices in the network there is the rule: **'When in doubt ask the SUC'.**

In order to play the role of the central entity to inform all others about the latest status of the network

- the SUCs Node-ID needs to be known by all nodes in the network,
- all changes of the network must be reported to the SUC,
- all nodes that store routes (controllers and routing slaves) must have a valid route to the SUC to ask for updates when needed and
- the SUC needs to be awake and ready to answer questions all the time.

The last requirement limits the SUC function to controllers that are mains powered and are always awake and always in the same physical location. No portable device or battery operated device can act as SUC.

Figure 3.31 shows a network with a SUC present that is informing all other devices about changes in the routing table and the configuration of the network.

Having an active SUC in the network allows the user to keep the primary controller role on a portable controller. Every change in the network caused by inclusion or exclusion of a node by the primary controller will be reported to the SUC and is then available to all other controllers, even if the primary controller is not active (see Figure 3.32).

Since remote controllers are typically battery-operated and therefore not active all the time, these controllers have to request an updated routing table periodically or at least when woken up by pressing a button. To perform this task, the mobile battery-operated controllers need to be informed about the presence of a SUC in the network.

If the original mobile battery-operated primary controller is lost or damaged, the SUC can assign the primary privilege to a new mobile controller, protecting the user from re-establishing the

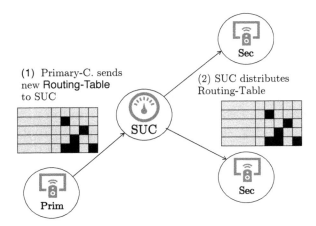

Figure 3.31: SUC in a Z-Wave-Network

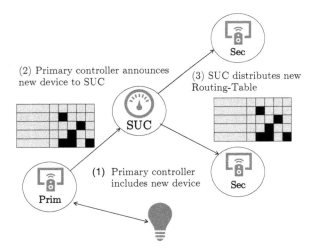

Figure 3.32: Update of the Routing table in a SUC

whole network with a brand new primary controller and having a different Home-ID.

Static ID Server (SIS)

The idea of the SIS (Static ID Server) is to allow multiple controllers to include devices. This is very convenient, particularly in larger networks and particularly in a network with multiple remote controls. The update function of new devices in the routing table is already solved by the SUC. The only remaining problem to overcome when using multiple controllers to include new devices is the maintenance of the Node-IDs. There needs to be one central instance that keeps track of issued and available Node-IDs. The SIS plays that role.

The SIS acts as depot for new Node-IDs that can be assigned by mobile controllers. Having an SIS present in the network allows every controller in the network to include further devices. The included controller requests a new Node-ID from the SIS first and then assigns this new Node-ID to the device being included. The SIS makes sure that a Node-ID gets never assigned to two nodes at the same time. A model of a SIS server in a Z-Wave network is presented in Figure 3.33.

Thanks to this, SIS all controllers can now include other nodes. In the Z-Wave language controllers in a network with an SIS present are called **inclusion controller**.

3.5.2   Explorer Frame

The explorer frame is a powerful tool to overcome communication problems in a network caused by incorrect network and routing information.

The explorer frame is a special frame that is sent out as a broadcast and is routed forward by every node in the network supporting the explorer frame process. This process is sometimes referred to as flooding. Of course, there needs to be a pruning

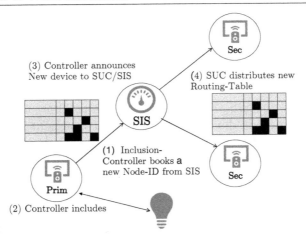

(3) Controller announces
New device to SUC/SIS

(4) SUC distributes new
Routing-Table

(1) Inclusion-
Controller books a
new Node-ID from SIS

(2) Controller includes

Figure 3.33: SIS Server in a Z-Wave network

mechanism to stop the forwarding to make sure the network does not get overloaded with repeatedly forwarded and broadcasted messages.

The explorer frame has a source address but no destination address. Every node forwarding the explorer frame adds its own Node-Id to the frame. Figure 3.35 shows the format of the explorer frame with additional 8 Bytes reserved for the routing detection function. If there is at least one valid route from the sender to its desired destination, the explorer frame will eventually reach this destination now carrying all the routing nodes used on its way. This information is the new and also the best route from the given source to the given destination. Figure 3.35 shows this principle. In the first step node 6 - the one that has lost the route - sends the explorer frame to node 5 and 7. Node 7 will terminate the explorer frame because it has no other routes available than the route back to node 6. Node 5 will now proceed the frame in a second step to nodes 4 and 3. After the third step, the explorer frame reaches the controller node 1 from node

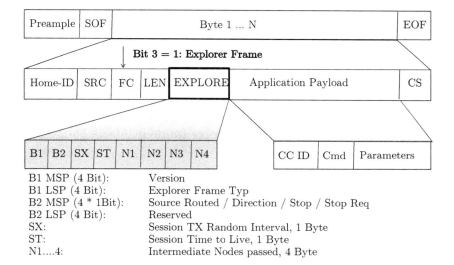

Figure 3.34: Explorer frame Layout

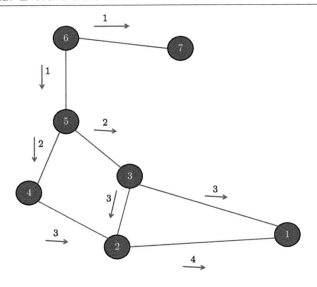

Figure 3.35: Explorer frame in Action

3, while node 2 receives two frames from 4 and 3. In the final step, node 2 will forward the frame to node 1 the only node that this node 2 did not get a frame before. However, node 1 will disregard this frame since it already knows the best valid route $1 \rightarrow 3 \rightarrow 5 \rightarrow 6$.

The receiver—in this case the controller—is now supposed to send the explorer frame information back to the sender using the route just detected. The sender receives this very valuable information and can update its routing table accordingly. Because the explorer frame generates a lot of network traffic, it is only used as the last resort after all other communication attempts fail. On the other hand, the explorer frame technology will find always a valid way if there is a valid way.

3.5.3   Explorer frames versus SUC/SIS in one network

Explorer frames and the SUC/SIS architecture can work in parallel in a network. Explorer Frame support typically also means support of SUC/SIS. However legacy devices with SUC/SIS support may not support explorer frames. If both approaches are supported, the network will automatically choose the option that is appropriate and able to handle the problem. The main difference between the two approaches can be summarized like:

- **Explorer frames will always find a valid way in the network without any further help by users as long as there is a way.**
- **SUC/SIC helps devices to find a way but there are some actions to be done in order to make this help effective. Nevertheless, certain limits to this help still apply.**

The limit in a SUC/SIS architecture without explorer frames are:

1. Inclusion and Exclusion must be done in *"direct range"*. These two commands require that the controller and the device to be excluded or included must be in direct wireless range. A SIS in the network allows every controller in the network to include and exclude devices. Nevertheless, the controller performing the action must be in *"direct range"* too.

2. Whenever there is a change in the network either adding devices, removing devices or moving devices (this does not apply to portable controllers that were designed to be portable), a network rediscovery is needed.

3. A special challenge is posed by battery-operated devices because they do not update their routing table until they wake up the next time. The usual solution is to keep the network rediscovery process active for a much longer time than required and hope that the battery-operated devices will wake up during this time to identify themselves with

their new position in the network.

How to know if a device supports explorer frames?

Unless the manual states support for explorer frames, the firmware version of the device needs to be checked. Device firmware is built using an SDK (Systems Development Kit) provided by Silicon Labs. The Z-Wave Alliance Product Database mentioned in Appendix A gives information about the firmware version used and also indicates if explorer frames are used. The following SDK versions support explorer frames:

- Every SDK Version 6.0 and up
- All SDKs between Version 4.5 and 4.9

In case the controller software does not show the SDK version during inclusion the following rules of thumb may help:

- If a device supports network wide inclusion it will also support explorer frames (for more information about network wide inclusion refer to chapter 5.1.5).
- If a device supports auto inclusion it will also support explorer frames.
- All Z-Wave Plus devices support explorer frame (for information about Z-Wave Plus please refer to chapter 1.6.4)
- All products launched prior to 2010 will not support explorer frame
- Most of the devices launched between 2010 and 2014 support explorer frame.
- All devices launched after 2014 support explorer frame

Table 3.8 summarizes the user actions needed and therefore the "convenience level" of the different ways to rediscover a Z-Wave network. Clearly only networks with complete explorer frame support are truly plug'n play.

Action	no SUC/SIS	SUC/SIS	explorer frames
Inclusion and Exclusion	primary controller must be in direct range	a controller must be in direct range	**no limitations**, device can be everywhere
Mains powered device moves in network	Network reconfig. mandatory plus updating of all routes impacted by moving node	Network reconfirmation required to update SUC, other update will happen automatically	**no user action needed**
Battery powered slave device moves in network	not supported	may be healed under certain circumstances	**no user action required**
Multiple Controllers in Network	controllers must be updated, action required after changes in network	**no user action required**	**no user action required**

Table 3.8: Comparison of different Z-Wave network management modes

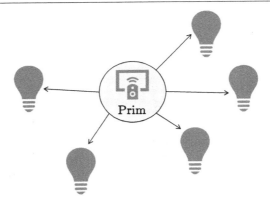

Figure 3.36: Z-Wave Network with one portable controller

3.6 Network configurations

3.6.1 Z-Wave Network with one portable controller

Z-Wave can work by starting with a very small network and extending this network later on as needed. A typical small network consists of a remote control and a couple of switches or dimmers. The remote control acts as the primary controller and both includes and controls the switches and dimmers. Before inclusion the dimmers and switches should be installed in their final location to make sure that a correct list of neighbors will be recognized and reported. Figure 3.36 shows a Z-Wave Network with one portable controller.

A network configuration like this works well as long as the remote control can reach all switches and dimmers directly (the node which is to be controlled is in a wireless range). In case the controlled node is not in range, the user may experience delays because the remote control needs to detect the network structure and calculate a route first before controlling the device. In case a device was included and moved afterwards to a new position, this

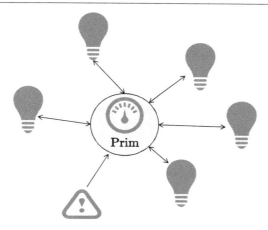

Figure 3.37: Example of a network with one static controller

particular device can only be controlled by the remote control if it is in direct range. Otherwise the communication will fail, because the routing table entry for this particular device is wrong and only few remote controls are able to do a network rediscovery.

This configuration is however not well suited for using battery operated devices since the portable controller is not able to handle wakeup interval communication.

3.6.2   Z-Wave Network with one static controller

Another typical network consists of a static controller (see Figure 3.37). This configuration is usually found if networks are controlled by a central controller or IP gateway.

The static controller is the primary controller and manages all other devices in the network. The actors can even send status updates to the controller.

Static controllers usually act as SUC and as SIS (for more information about SUC and SIS please refer to chapter 3.5.1 and

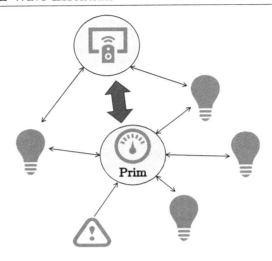

Figure 3.38: Z-Wave network with a static and a portable controller

3.5.1). This ensures a stable and well-managed network with a mixture of mains and battery operated devices. If devices are moved with the range of the network the network will automatically update the routing tables and ensure fast and error-free routing. Even without a SUC a network can operate in stable condition as long as there is no change of the position of devices. In case a device was moved the user need to perform a network re-organization.

Figure 3.37 shows the configuration of a network with a static controller and mains and battery operated devices.

3.6.3 Portable and static controller in one network

If there are more than one controller in the network, only one of them can act as a primary controller and all other controllers become secondary controllers. The user may choose which controller is what depending on personal preferences. A portable primary controller is convenient for inclusion and exclusion of devices but bear the danger that the device can get lost. A static controller is a safe bet but may make inclusion and exclusion of devices less convenient.

In case these are battery-operated devices in the network, the static controller should be used for inclusion and exclusion. This ensures that all battery-operated devices are configured properly and allow minimization of battery consumption during operation. Some static controllers allow reconfiguring the device when included by a different device. In case the static controller can act as SUC/SIS the portable controller can be used as inclusion controller. The SUC/SIS will then make sure all battery operated devices are configured correctly. Figure 3.38 shows a network configuration that mixes static and portable controller.

3.6.4   Network with SUC/SIS controller

As soon as there are multiple portable controllers in a network, a static controller with SUC/SIS function becomes mandatory. Otherwise, all controllers need to be updated manually every time one of the controllers has included or excluded a device. Thanks to the SUC, this update happens automatically and without any manual interaction, and all battery-operated devices are also configured properly. Figure 3.39 shows such a configuration.

3.6.5   Comparison of different network configurations

Table 3.9 summarizes the insights on the different network configurations:

It is safe to assume that all contemporary static controllers can function as SUC and SIS. This shortens the list of requirements for valid and recommended network configurations:

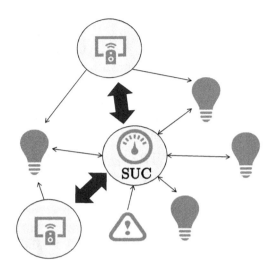

Figure 3.39: Z-Wave Network with SUC

Configuration	SUC needed	battery operated device
portable controller only	No	No
static controller only	No	Yes
static and portable controller together	No but recommended	must be configured by static controller
multiple portable and a static controller	Yes	must be configured by static controller
multiple static controller	Yes	Configuration Problems

Table 3.9: Different valid network configurations

1. In case there is only a portable controller don't use battery operated devices.

2. In case there is a mix of static and portable controllers please use the static controller for inclusion, particularly for battery operated devices. This ensures that the battery-operated devices are configured correctly.

3. In case there are multiple static controllers make sure to use only one of them for inclusion and network management and don't switch between them.

Chapter 4

Z-Wave Application Layer

So far, we have only looked at how different nodes can communicate with each other. The application layer of the Z-Wave protocol now defines and specifies **what and why** two nodes communicate with each other.

4.1   Devices and Commands

4.1.1   Types of Z-Wave Devices

In theory, every controllable or controlling device in a home or office can be equipped with Z-Wave technology. Hence, one should expect a broad variety of different devices and functions. However, there are some basic functionality patterns that allow categorizing different devices.

Each device will either control other devices or being controlled by other devices. In the Z-Wave terminology controlling devices are called **controllers**, reporting devices are called **sensors** and controlled devices are called **actors or actuators**. It is also possible to combine a logical sensor controller or actor function

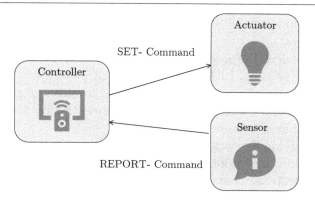

Figure 4.1: Z-Wave Controllers, Sensors and Actors

within one physical device. Figure 4.1 shows the three basic device types.

Actors switch either digital (on/off for an electrical switch) or analogue signals (0% ... 100% for a dimmer or window blind control). Sensors deliver either a digital signal (door, glass breaking, motion detector, window button on the wall) or an analogue signal (temperature, humidity, power).

In today's market of Z-Wave devices, there is a surprisingly short list of different product categories. Nearly all Z-Wave devices on the market can be categorized into one of the following function groups:

1. Electrical switches are designed either as plug-in modules for wall outlets or as replacements for traditional wall switches (digital actors). It is also possible to have these actors already built into certain electrical appliances such as electrical stoves or heaters.

2. Electrical dimmers, either as plug-in modules for wall outlets or as replacements for traditional wall dimmers (analogue actors).

3. Motor control, usually to open or close a door, a window, a

window sun blind or a Venetian blind (analogue or digital actors).

4. Electrical Displays or other kind of user interface devices such as siren, LED panel, etc. (digital actors).

5. Measuring Sensors of different kind to measure parameters like temperature, humidity, gas concentration (e.g. carbon dioxide or carbon monoxide).

6. Notifying Sensors of different kind to indicate digital information (e.g. door contact or motion detection).

7. Thermostat controls: either as a one knob control or using a temperature display (analogue sensors).

8. Heating and cooling controls such as TRVs (Thermostat Radiator Valves) or floor heating controls (analogue or digital actors).

9. Remote Controls either as universal remote control with IR support or as dedicated Z-Wave Remote Control with special keys for network functions, group and/or scene control.

10. IP Gateways or other central controllers like USB sticks with PC software allowing users to access Z-Wave networks. Using IP communication these interfaces also allow remote access over the Internet.

11. Door locks of various kinds.

In Z-Wave Plus, there is a defined list of device types every products needs to fit in. They basically mirror the list given above. The Z-Wave Plus device types also define what network role types the product has to follow. For example, a power switch must always be an "Always-on-Slave." For more information about Z-Wave Plus Network Role Types, please refer to Chapter 3.3.3. This is the complete list of Z-Wave Plus–defined device types for smart homes:

1. Central Controller and Sub System Controller

2. Display - Simple

3. Door Lock Keypad, as Deadbolt or Lever

4. Fan Switch

5. Light Dimmer Switch
6. On/Off Power Switch and Power Strip
7. Remote Control, as AV, Multi-Purpose or Simple
8. Sensor
9. Set Top Box and TV
10. Siren
11. Sub Energy Meter
12. Thermostat, HVAC or Setback
13. Valve, open/close
14. Wall Controller
15. Whole Home Energy Meter, Advanced or Simple
16. Window Covering, as "No Position/Endpoint", "Endpoint Aware" or "Position/Endpoint Aware"

4.1.2   Command Classes

Every message that is exchanged between Z-Wave devices is called a command. Commands can be classified into three major categories:

- ask a device to do something (`Set`)
- ask a device to provide something (`Get`)
- report a certain value or status to a device (`Report`)

According to the different device types, the `Set`, `Get` and `Report` commands may mean different things and need to be specified further.

Z-Wave organizes all the commands in the so-called **Command Classes**. Command classes describe a certain function of a device and group all necessary commands to deal with this function.

Example 1: the battery function

If a device wants to deal with the battery function of another device there is no clear meaning of a `Set` command, since there is nothing to set for a remote battery. Clearly a `Get` command makes sense since there may be a need to ask for a battery status value or the actual battery draw. Since these values need to be reported the **Report** command is required as well.

This pretty much describes a Z-Wave command class called **Battery**. The battery command class knows two commands:

- **Get()** ... ask a device to report its actual charging status
- **Report(value)** ... the actual charging status is reported.

The different functions of different devices require a long list of command classes that reach from lighting control via heating to door locks and beyond.

Example 2: a simple switch

A normal on/off switch is referred to as a binary switch. The basic function of a binary switch is to turn a switch on and off. A Z-Wave controller may also want to know the status of the switch, hence a status request function and a status report function is required too.

- **Set(value)**: is sent from a controller to the switch to turn the switch on or off.
- **Get()**: is sent from the controller to the switch to request a report about the switching state.
- **Report(value)**: is sent from the switch back to the controller as a response to the Get Command.

These three commands and responses are grouped and referred to as command class **Binary Switch**. If a certain Z-Wave device supports the command class **Binary Switch**, it is supposed to be able to deal with all these commands:

- The switch needs to understand the set command and set the switch accordingly.
- The switch is able to receive a get command and is able to response with a report command in the proper format.

Figure 4.2 shows some examples of Z-Wave command classes. Most but not all of them support one or more of the basic commands **Set**, **Get** and **Report** and other more specific commands.

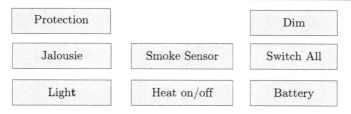

Figure 4.2: Examples of different command classes

Example 3: a dimmer

A dimming function can certainly be realized with the three basic functions **Set**, **Get** and **Report**. **Set** will allow to set a dimmer level, **Get** asks for the actual dimming level and **Report** sends the actual dimming level.

However, there is also a need for a command to start the dimming process and to stop the dimming process to emulate the behavior of a normal wall dimmer or window control: Keeping a button pushed moves the window in a certain direction or starts dimming; releasing the button stops moving or dimming. Hence, the command class **Multilevel Switch**, that controls a dimmer has two additional commands: DIM **START(direction)** and DIM **STOP()**.

Command classes are identified by a single byte number. Annex C shows the complete list of command classes by ID.

The commands within the command class are identified by a single byte number as well. This leads to the command class layout as shown in Figure 4.3.

In case there are no further values to transmit, the smallest possible command class has a length of 2 bytes. Most of the commands however are larger in size.

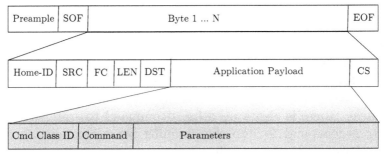

Cmd Class ID: ID of the command class, 1 Byte
Command: Command of Command Class (e.g. SET)
Parameters: Additional parameters or variables

Figure 4.3: Frame Layout for Command Classes

4.1.3 Command Class `Basic`

There is one very special command class called `Basic`. `Basic` is a wildcard command class. It is not tied to a special device function but just offers the three very basic commands:

- `Set`: set a value between 0 and 255 (0x00 .. 0xff);
- `Get`: ask the device to report a value;
- `Report`: response to the Get command. Reports a value between 0 and 255 (0x00 .. 0xff).

The specialty of the `Basic` command class is that every device will interpret the basic commands dependent of its specific functionality:

- A binary switch will switch on when receiving a value 255 and switch off when receiving a value of 0;
- A thermostat may turn into a convenience temperature mode when receiving value = 0 and may turn into an energy-saving mode when receiving a higher value;
- A temperature sensor will issue a basic report and send an integer temperature value;
- A door sensor will either send out a value = 0 in case the door is closed or a 255 (0xff) when the door is opened.

The basic command class as shown in Figure 4.4 is the smallest common denominator of all Z-Wave devices. Every Z-Wave device must support the `Basic` command class; however, certain commands may be ignored if there is no meaningful implementation in the device.

4.1.4 Device Classes

To allow interoperability between different Z-Wave devices from different manufacturers, certain Z-Wave devices must have certain well-defined functions above and beyond the basic command class. The structure behind these requirements is called a **device class**. A device class refers to certain device types and defines which command classes are mandatory to support. There are

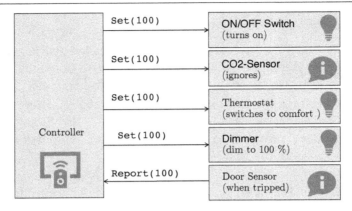

Figure 4.4: **Basic** Command Class

three levels of device class specifications:

- Every device must belong to a **basic device class**.
- Devices can be further specified by assigning them to a **generic device class**.
- Further functionality can be defined as assigning the device to a **specific device class**.

Basic Device Class

The basic device class makes a distinction merely whether the device is a controller (mobile or static) or a slave. Therefore, every device belongs to one basic device class.

Generic Device Class

The generic device class defines the basic function a device is supposed to offer as a controller or slave. A list of device classes is available in Annex B.

Specific Device Class

Assigning a specific device class to a Z-Wave device allows to further specify the functionality of the device. Assigning a specific device class is voluntary and only makes sense, if the device really supports all specific functions of a specific device class. Special device classes are, for example:

- Setback Thermostat (SETBACK THERMOSTAT) is a specific device class of the generic device class Thermostat;
- Multi-level Power Switch (MULTILEVEL POWER SWITCH) is a specific device class of the generic device class MULTILEVEL SWITCH.

Once a Z-Wave device is assigned to a specific device class, it is required to support a set of command classes as functions of this specific device class. These required command classes are called **mandatory command classes** and they comprise certain generic and specific device classes. Above and beyond the mandatory device classes, Z-Wave devices can support further **optional command classes**. These optional command classes may be very useful but the standard does not enforce the implementation of them. However, some command classes are recommended in the standard to be implemented. They are called **recommended command classes**.

A Z-Wave manufacturer is allowed to implement an unlimited number of optional device classes. However, if these device classes are implemented, the standard defines how these commands and functions are to be supported. The recommended and mandatory command classes within a device class can be seen in Figure 4.1.4.

The basic device class, the generic device class, and, if available, the specific device class are announced by the device during inclusion, using a **Node Information Frame** (for more information about Node Information Frame please refer to

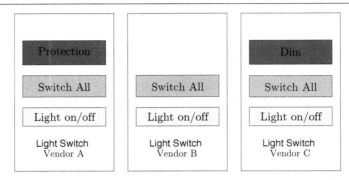

Figure 4.6: Different Implementation of a Device Class Binary Power Switch by different vendors

chapter 4.2.1). Beside the device classes, the Node Information Frame also announces all optional command classes of the device included. With this announcement, a controller can control and use an included Z-Wave device according to its functionality. Figure 4.6 shows the different implementation of a Device Class "Binary Power Switch" by different vendors with some mandatory and some optional command classes.

A Z-Wave device works according to the Z-Wave standard if

- It belongs to a basic device class and a generic device class and is able to report these classes on request using a Node Information Frame.
- It supports all mandatory command classes of the basic and generic command class by sending commands and reports as well as accepting and executing commands according specification of the command class.

- In case a specific device class is defined, the mandatory command classes of this specific device class need to be supported as well and the specific device class needs to be reported on request.
- In case optional command classes are implemented, these command classes need to be announced in the Node Information Frame on request and need to be supported according to the Z-Wave command class specifications.
- In case the device shall be a Z-Wave Plus device it must announce this in a specific command class `Z-Wave Plus Indicator`. Within this command class the device must choose a valid Network Role Type and a valid Device Type.

Z-Wave defines a broad variety of command classes covering almost every aspect of home automation and control. Nevertheless, it is possible that manufacturers want to implement further functionality not already defined in a command class specification.

The command class `proprietary function` is available to cover this need. A proprietary function would allow a manufacturer to implement specific functions that can then be used only by other devices supporting this proprietary function as well.

The use of a proprietary function is subject to approval by the Z-Wave Alliance certification authority and is required to be documented extensively. So far only very few devices make use of this function indicating that the current Z-Wave specification is quite complete. Typically, new requirements result sooner or later in an amendment to the existing standard, which makes this function part of the official standard and any proprietary extension becomes obsolete.

One example shall illustrate the use of device classes and command classes:

Example: Definition of a Wall Plug A manufacturer wants to offer a plug-

in switch as shown in Figure 4.1.4. The basic function of this switch is switching the power on and off. Since such a device can be used at multiple locations, the basic device class **Routing Slave** is used. As a binary switch the device belongs to the generic device class **Binary Switch**. It is allowed and in this case even recommended to use a specific device class **Binary Power Switch** since this plug-in switch will always switch power lines.

- Basis class: **Routing Slave**
- Generic class: **Binary Switch**
- Special class: **Binary Power Switch**

1. The **Binary Switch** device class requires the implementation of the mandatory command class **Binary Switch** and, of course, the implementation of the **Basic** command class.

2. As binary power switch, the device is furthermore requested to implement the so-called **Switch-All** command class. This command class defines the reaction of a device when receiving a **Switch-All** command that can be sent from a controller to all devices in the network. (The purpose of this command is to quickly shut down or bring up all electrical loads in a home.) The **Switch-All** command class allows defining under which circumstances a device should react to this **Switch-All** command issued by the controller. A generic switch is not required to implement such a command class but ignore the **Switch-All** command, since an **All-Off** command may not mean something useful to a generic switch. In case of a power switch an **All-Off** com-

mand is clearly defined and therefore a mandatory command class.

3. If the device shall be certified as Z-Wave Plus Device the manufacturer has to pick a Network Role and a Device Type and add the `Z-Wave Info` Command Class, which indicates the compliance with Z-Wave Plus. In this case, it would be the Network Role Type `'Always One Slave'` and the Device Type `'On/Off Power Switch'`.

It is allowed by the standard not to implement the `Switch-All` command class but in this case the device is not allowed to announce a specific device class `Binary Power Switch`. A switching device without `Switch-All` support that just announces a generic device class `Binary Switch` would still be a valid Z-Wave compliant device.

- The manufacturer wants to offer more a competitive product and adds further functionality to the switching device. One may be the so-called 'child protection command class'. A child protection function on a binary switch means the ability to disable local control capability and only allow switching the device wirelessly. If the manufacturer decides to implement such a function the standard defines in the `Protection` command class how to do this. Also, the optional command class `Protection` needs to be announced in the Node Information Frame.

- The manufacturer may decide to further enhance the switch by offering a special function, which randomly switches the device on and off. In conjunction with a lamp this function may be used as anti-theft device in the home. There is presently no command class defining such a capability. The manufacturer could now ask for approval to implement this function and still be certified as a Z-Wave-compliant device. Depending on the approval, the function would be realized as proprietary function.

4.2   Managing Devices

4.2.1   Node Information Frame

Each Z-Wave device belongs to a certain device class and is therefore able to support certain command classes. **The Node Information Frame (NIF)** is a special message a device can send out to inform other devices about its own capabilities. The node information frame contains the following information:

- Basic Device Class
- Generic Device Class
- Specific Device Class
- Information if the device is mains powered, battery-operated or FLiRS
- In case it is a FLiRS device, the wakeup frequency (250 ms or 1s)
- A list of all Command Classes the device supports
- Optionally a list of all Command Classes the device is controlling

Figure 4.8 shows the format of the Node Information Frame. **The Node information frame is like a business card of the Z-Wave device.** It's used whenever there is a need to announce itself:

- for inclusion into a network.
- for exclusion out of a network.
- when associations are set (for association please refer to chapter 4.2.7).
- when associations are deleted.
- sometime to announce that the device is awake.

Every Z-Wave device must have a way to send out a Node Information Frame (NIF). Every device manufacturer has the freedom how to trigger a Node Information Frame being sent. Commonly used implementations are:

- a dedicated button on the outer enclosure of the device or sometimes inside the device.

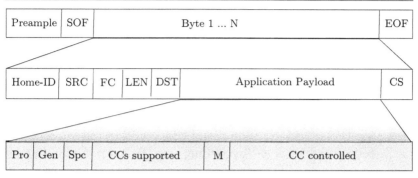

Pro: Protocol Flags
Gen: Generic Device Class
Spc: Specific Device Class
CC support:List of supported Command Classes
CC control: List of controlled Command Classes (optional)
M: Mark Byte (0xFE)

Figure 4.8: Node Information Frame

- a tamper protection button, typically for PIR and other sensors.
- using the switch paddle of a wall switch.
- using a magnet to switch a magnet sensor inside the device, used when there is no space left or the enclosure is water protected and therefore a button is not suitable.

Because the Node Information Frame is such a universal way to announce the presence of a device the manuals may not explicitly refer to the function. They may refer to a confirmation of inclusion (that means sending out a Node Information Frame) or confirmation of an association (again, on network level this means sending out a Node Information Frame).

In Z-Wave Plus the NIF must show the special **Z-Wave Plus Command Class**-ID as very first command class. This is the indicator that the device complies to Z-Wave Plus.

4.2.2   Interview

During the inclusion process every Z-Wave device sends out its Node Information Frame to the including device, the controller. The controller now knows what kind of device was included. It knows the command classes that are supported and is already able to use the device.

However, certain information is embedded in the command classes and needs to be received by issuing specific commands of these command classes. These commands are referred to as **interview commands**. The device interview process is demonstrated in Figure 4.2.2.

Example 1

The command class meter allows receiving meter values. For this purpose, a `GET()` command is used. The command class, however, allows specifying what kind of meter values can be reported.

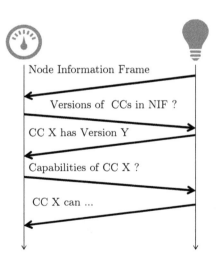

If a controller understands that the device is supporting the meter command class, the controller may send the device a command called `SUP-PORTED-GET()` to receive a `SUPPORTED-REPORT()`. This report contains a list of all meter values (W, kWh, m3/h, m3, BTU and others) the meter is metering.

Example 2

The `WAKEUP` command class allows setting the wakeup interval for a battery-operated

Figure 4.9: Device Interview Process

device. It allows to issue a
SET(wakeup interval) or a
GET() that causes the device
to report the actual wakeup
interval. However, the device can also report a desired
wakeup interval. The controller can now decide to just set a certain wakeup interval of choice to the device or to ask the device
for its desired value in order to take this into account.

For more information about the Interview process please refer to
Chapter 5.1.9.

4.2.3 Configuration

The Z-Wave standard defines that every device shall be functional
on factory defaults right after inclusion. Nevertheless, there are
devices that may require further user and application specific
setups such as

- sensitivity of a motion detector,
- behavior of control LED lights,
- switching delay of an alarm sensor or
- specific behavior under error conditions.

The configuration of a device is performed using the optional
command class Configuration. The configuration command
class allows the setting of up to 255 parameters with one value
each. Configurations are device specific and all parameters and
possible values need to be described in the devices manual.

In order to do a configuration, the user needs to know the configuration parameter number and the desired value.

Example: Configuration of a status LED on a device

Parameter No. 2: switches the LED on the device on, off or
blinking according to the status of the device

- Value = 0: Always off

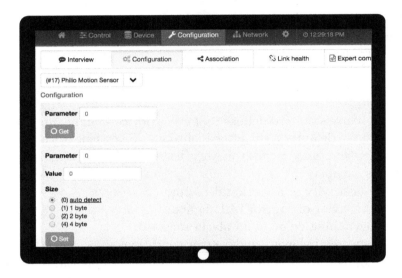

Figure 4.10: Example of a generic configuration interface in PC Software (Source: Expert User Interface of Z-Way by z-wave.me)

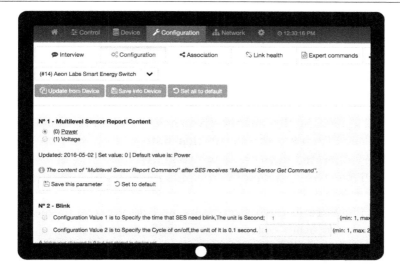

Figure 4.11: Example of a user-friendly configuration interface in PC Software (Source: Expert User Interface of Z-Way by z-wave.me)

- Value = 1: Blinks when active
- Value = 2: Always on

Configurations are typically done using static controllers (PC software, wall panel or an IP gateway). The generic configuration interface according to Figure 4.10 requires the knowledge about the configuration parameter numbers and the meaning of the values to be stored. This information is required to be given in the manual of the device or in the Z-Wave Alliance Product Database referred to in Annex A.

Modern and more user-friendly installation tools maintain a database of known devices with their configuration parameters and possible values. They provide a translation of the values into human-readable explanation, thus making configuration much easier. Figure 4.11 shows an example of a user interface with readable explanations of configuration parameters.

For more information about the Interview process please refer to Chapter 5.1.10.

4.2.4   Battery Management

Battery-operated devices are a special challenge within a Z-Wave network, because they are mostly in a deep sleep state and cannot be reached from a controller in this state.

Battery-operated devices know two states:

- They are awake and can communicate with other devices of the network.
- They are in deep sleep state and do not communicate at all. To other controllers they may appear as non-existing or damaged.

In order to allow communication with battery-operated devices, a mains-powered and therefore always active static controller needs to maintain a waiting queue, where all commands are stored that are to be sent to a sleeping device. When the battery-operated device wakes up, it informs this controller and requests the information held in the mailbox.

At the moment, a battery-operated device wakes up it sends a so-called **WAKEUP -NOTIFICATION** to the controller and stays awake. The WAKEUP-NOTIFICATION indicates to the controller that the battery device is now listening to commands. If all commands are sent, the controller will send a final command **NO-MORE-INFO** to indicate to the battery device that it can go back to deep sleep mode. If the battery-operated device does not receive a NO-MORE-INFO, it will go back to deep sleep mode after a defined time, maximum 10 seconds. This process of sleeping and wakeup is demonstrated in Figure 4.12.

Most battery-operated devices will have an internal timer, which wakes up the device regularly to check for queued commands. This sleeping interval time must be configured. A typical sleeping interval is between 30 seconds and several days and can usually

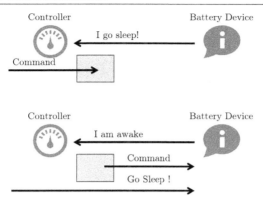

Figure 4.12: Sleeping and wakeup

be configured on a user interface of the controller. Any change of the wakeup time will, like any other command sent to the battery device, become effective after the next wakeup.

Certain devices limit the wakeup interval to a maximum and minimum value, and ignore wakeup intervals that are out of these allowed limits. Figure 4.13 shows an example of a wakeup time dialog.

To allow an initial configuration of a device after inclusion every battery device shall stay awake for a defined time afterwards. This time may vary between 20 seconds and some minutes.

Table 4.1 summarized the different states of a battery-operated device and the conditions to change the status.

4.2.5   Maximization of battery lifetime

Devices with wakeup interval

Battery lifetime is the critical measure of battery-operated devices. Therefore, some estimates should be given and considered.

- A typical Alkaline-Microcell (AA) as shown in Figure 4.14

Figure 4.13: Example of a wakeup time dialog (Source: Expert User Interface of Z-Way by z-wave.me)

Figure 4.14: AAA Battery

Situation	Awake	Sleeping
Inclusion	Right after inclusion	Turns into sleeping mode after a couple of minutes without any further user action.
Regularly	Wakes up after a defined interval and sends a notification to static controller. Typical wakeup intervals are between minutes and hours and can be configured by the user within certain boundaries	Controller can turn back the battery-operated device by sending a command. Otherwise the battery device turns back into sleeping mode after a defined time (usually 10 seconds)
Local operation of the device	Wakes up on every local operation and communicates status if needed (e.g. button pressed)	Immediately after finishing action

Table 4.1: Conditions to change state for battery-operated devices

IC Generation	Hibernate	CPU active	RX on	TX on
100	31 μA		23mA	25 mA
200 (since 2005)	2.5 μA		21 mA	36 mA
300 (since 2007)	2.5 μA	10 mA	23 mA	36 mA (0 dbm)
400 (since 2009)	1.5 μA		23 mA	36 mA
500 (since 2013)	1 μA	15 mA	32 mA	34 mA (0 dbm)
700 (since 2018)	¡ 1 μA	¡ 3 mA	6mA	6 mA (6 dbm)

Table 4.2: Power consumptions of different chip generation

has an energy capacity of approx. 1000 mAh. A typical battery-operated sensor has 2 such batteries to provide 3 V operating voltage.

- A Z-Wave module that uses the very popular Series 500 chip consumes 1μA in the deep sleep state and 32 mA in the wakeup mode. During transmission of packets about 34 mA are required (on 3 Volt). Table 4.2 shows the current need of the Series 500 chip generations in their respective working conditions.

- Additional battery power can be used for the devices functionality such as operating an infrared sensor or moving a thermostat valve. This power consumption varies from device to device and is usually minor compared to the power used for the electronics. For the following estimate this portion of the power usage will be neglected.

If a sensor is in the active reception mode, the battery is empty after

$$1000 \text{ mAh} / 32 \text{ mA} = 30 \text{ hours} = 1.5 \text{ days}$$

Wakeup interval	Battery life time
120 Seconds	23 days
5 Minutes (typical)	59 days
30 Minutes	357 days
24 hours	46 years

Table 4.3: Battery lifetime if no static controller is present (for Series 500 ICs)

It is therefore mandatory to move a battery-operated device into the deep sleep state for most of the time. The maximum battery lifetime in the deep sleep state is

$$1000 \text{ mAh} / 0.001 \text{ mA} = 1.000.000 \text{ hours} = 41.666 \text{ days} = 113 \text{ years.}$$

By this time, even alkaline batteries will have become empty by self-discharging.

Usually a battery-operated device will wake up, send a wakeup notification, and wait for command from the controller including the final command (`no more info`) to go back in deep sleep. If no commands arrive (because the static controller is not reachable or not present or turned down), it is recommended by Z-Wave to keep the device awake for 10 seconds and go back to deep sleep state automatically. The wakeup interval—this means the time between two wakeup events–will determine the battery lifetime as shown in Table 4.3. These numbers assume the device is kept awake for the maximum time of 10 seconds.

A battery lifetime of 59 days (ignoring of all local operations like blinking of a LED, moving of a motor etc.!) is still not acceptable. It is therefore very important to keep the static controller in the network to quickly answer all wakeup notifications and shorten the wakeup time of the battery-operated devices.

Table 4.4 shows the battery lifetime with some typical wakeup intervals under the assumption, that the controller is able to send

Wakeup interval Battery	lifetime
120 Seconds	4 Years
5 Minutes (typical)	10 Years
30 Minutes	29 Years
24 Hours	45 Years

Table 4.4: Battery lifetime with active static controller (for Series 500 ICs, 1000 mAh battery)

every device back into deep sleep state right after receiving the wakeup - notification.

It is quite obvious that the presence of a static controller significantly extends the battery lifetime of battery-operated devices with wakeup interval. Real battery lifetime will be substantially shorter since these calculations in Table 4.3 and 4.4 do not take into account

- the application will need to exchange messages (e.g. sending sensor value),
- the controller may not be able to answer the wakeup notification right away minimizing the awake time of the device,
- electronics of the battery operated device will take power as well,
- and self-discharging of the battery.

Typical battery lifetimes are between 2 and 5 years for devices with wakeup interval without heavy traffic.

Devices with FLiRS technology

FLiRS devices wake up every 250 ms or every 1 s. This wakeup interval is independent of the device state or any configuration command. When in deep sleep state the device consumed the amount of energy as shown in table 4.2. Although the wakeup time is very short the frequent wakeup still consumes same energy on average:

- Series 300 ICs: 80 μAh per hour.
- Series 500 ICs: 50 μAh per hour.

This energy consumption is a compromise between battery lifetime and delay in reaction when a wireless command is sent. It's also worth to mention that the transmitter may need considerable amount of energy to send the so-called wakeup beam for about 1 sec.

Assuming there is a battery of 1000 mAh, a FLiRS device will have - ignoring all other need for energy - 1000 mAh / 50 μ Ah / h = 20.000 h = 833 days = 2.5 years life with one battery. The real battery life will be even shorter since the device function - e.g. the motor turning a door lock also consumes energy.

4.2.6 Multichannel Devices

As long as a device has only one function of its kind (such as one switch, one sensor), the command class associated with this function will perfectly announce and control this function. However, there are devices that have multiple times the same function. A good example is an intelligent power strip with, let us say, 8 outlets, each controlled by an on/off switch. Just having one command class `Switch Binary()` will allow controlling all outlets together and not the individual ones. The solution to this problem is called **Multichannel Device**. With this command class Z-Wave introduces the concept of virtual sub devices. A command class `Multichannel Command Class` reported in the NIF indicates that the device supports multiple channels. The command class reports the number of channels and some other context information. A controller can now communicate with the different channels by encapsulating normal commands in a so-called 'channel wrapper'. This is a special command class that provided additional information as a header to the real application command. Figure 4.15 shows how a normal command is encapsulated in a multichannel command class.

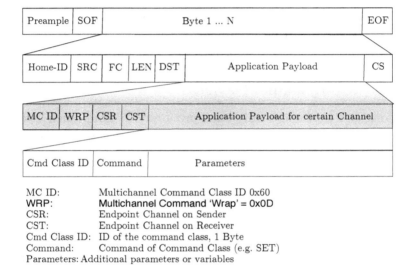

MC ID: Multichannel Command Class ID 0x60
WRP: **Multichannel Command 'Wrap' = 0x0D**
CSR: Endpoint Channel on Sender
CST: Endpoint Channel on Receiver
Cmd Class ID: ID of the command class, 1 Byte
Command: Command of Command Class (e.g. SET)
Parameters: Additional parameters or variables

Figure 4.15: Multichannel Command Class Encapsulation

Within the channel the device behaves like a normal Z-Wave device. It has a (Channel)-NIF and is supporting command classes. It is even possible to have different device types in different channels of the very same physical device.

A device can have up to 127 different channels. However, channels are only used if more than one similar function is implemented in one physical device.

The multichannel concept was introduced to Z-Wave quite late and it is not easy to implement. That is why some of the early Z-Wave controllers did not support it properly resulting in malfunctions when connecting to multichannel devices. As a backup, it is required to offer a basic function outside the channel in the normal context of the device—in their command classes. Z-Wave plus controllers must support multichannel devices.

4.2.7   Associations

An **association** defines a sensor → actor relationship within a network. It is defined as a structure

IF (... this and this happens ...) → **THEN** (... do this and that ...)

Some examples

> **IF** button 2 is pressed **THEN** ceiling lamp shall go on. **IF** temperature sensor goes above $22°C$, → **THAN** turn down the heating **AND** open the window.

In order to accomplish this kind of IF→ THEN relationship the following requirements need to be met:

- The actor device needs to be identified and able to perform the desired task.
- The sensor or controller needs to be able to generate an event that causes the action.

- The sensor or controller needs to know which actor to control in which way in case the event occurs.

The first requirement is quite obvious. If the ceiling light—to stay in the first example—will be turned on, the ceiling light needs to be controlled by a Z-Wave device that can be turned on and off wirelessly. While this sounds straightforward, there are plenty of examples where the actor is not able to fulfill the desired task, e.g. a dimming device cannot change the color of an LED light.

The second requirement is also obvious. There must be a defined event that causes an action. In case a button of a controller is involved, this is quite easy but for sensors that measure constant values this may become a challenge.

Binary sensors such as door sensors or motion detectors generate an event whenever their binary state changed from on (window open) to off (window closed). For a motion detector, it gets more complicated. The motion part, typically resulting in an ON-event is easy to detect but how about the OFF-event?

How can a motion detector be sure that there is no person in the room anymore? Most motion detectors allow to set a certain timeout value and generate an OFF event when the time has run out. It is also imaginable to do nothing after a given time. Even then the motion detector needs to know the minimum time between two events to be generated. Otherwise, it will constantly generate events that result in network traffic when a person moves in the room.

Timings and settings are typical configuration values of a motion detector and often can be changed either locally using buttons and/or wirelessly using the `Configuration` command class described in Chapter 4.2.3.

Sensors that measure an analog value such as temperature, CO_2 level, humidity, etc. cannot generate an event from just measuring the value. In case the device will be used to start an IF $(\dots) \rightarrow$ THEN $(\dots)$ association action, they need to know cer-

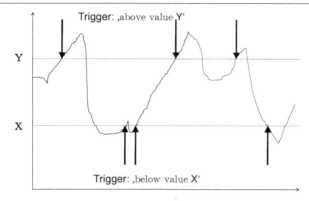

Figure 4.16: How a trigger works

tain boundaries of the measured values and what to do if the measured value reaches the boundary value set. The boundary values that are used to generate events are called **Trigger Levels**. Figure 4.16 shows how the crossing of a real value and the trigger level creates events.

The third condition is the real core of the association: Devices that can perform association (meaning controlling devices dependent on events) store the controlled devices in the so-called **association groups**.

> An association group refers to a certain event in the device and defines a group of devices that will receive a command in case this event happens (see Figure 4.17).

This means as an example that every button of a remote control must have at least one association group, because only then it is possible to define devices that shall be operated when the button is pressed.

Association groups are defined by three parameters:

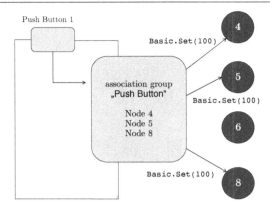

Figure 4.17: All nodes in an association group receive a signal when the event happens.

(1) What is the event?

There are a variety of possible events:

- pushing a button,
- tampering alarm for a security related product,
- reaching a defined trigger level for a measuring device,
- success or failure of a door lock opening event, etc.

In case of buttons it's even possible to have more than one association group:

1. One group may define the devices to be operated at a single click of the button.
2. One group may define the devices to be operated at a double click of the button.
3. One group may define the devices to be operated when two buttons are pressed.

The number of different association groups is a performance parameter of a given device. It is possible to keep the device simple and cheap by putting different events into one single association group (and let the actor devices find out what to do) or to have different groups for different events.

Special association group Lifeline

Z-Wave Plus has added a special association Group called **Lifeline**. Every Z-Wave Plus device must support the command class `association` and offer as a minimum one association group with No. 1. This group is not connected to any event of the device but devices in this group will receive all notifications and information relevant for a central controller.

This simplifies the work of central controllers and gateways. They always want to show the actual status of all devices in the network and therefore they must include themselves into all and every association group not to miss any information. With the Lifeline, this gets way less complicated. Devices are supposed to send every gateway-relevant information at least into the Lifeline to that the controller will only receive information from the Lifeline. Typical information sent into the Lifeline includes battery status notifications, alarm messages and heart beats. Sending `BASIC` control messages into the Lifeline only makes sense if the controller can refer them to a specific status or event on the device. For example, this would work for a simple door sensor that just knows on and off (`Basic.SET(0)` and `Basic.SET(1)`).

(2) How big is the group?

Due to memory restrictions, it is not possible to store all possible $232\text{-}1 = 231$ devices [1] in an association group. The number of devices is therefore limited. 5 or 12 devices are a very common number but there are also devices that have association groups with only one single possible device.

The number of association groups and the max. number of devices in an association group is very common information to be

---

[1] A Z-Wave network can address 232 devices and an association to the own device does not make sense

detected during the device interview described in chapter 4.2.2.

(3) What command should be sent?

Depending on the kind of actions to be performed, the kind of command should be different for each device.

To simplify the setup and management of association groups, most devices make the following two simplifications:

1. All devices in an association group are controlled by the command class `Basic.` (except for the special association group lifeline as explained above)
2. All devices in an association group receive the very same command. In case the `Basic` command class is used the value sent with `Basic.Set()` is identical for all devices in one association group.

There is a command class allowing to configure the type of command sent to devices in one Association Group. The name of the command class is already complicated: `Association Command Configuration` and the implementation is even worse. The result is that only very few devices take advantage of this command class to further specify the type and value of command.

However, certain binary sensors at least allow defining what value can be set in case the event happens or does not happen anymore.

Example

Default: Door sensor detects open → `Basic.Set(1)` is sent out, Door sensor closes again → `Basic.Set(0)` is sent out. A configuration value allows to turn this relationship to:

- open→ `Basic.Set(0)` and
- closed → `Basic.Set(1)`.

How association groups are managed?

Setting and deleting devices into or from association groups is best accomplished using a graphical user interface of a central controller. These user interface typically show a list of association groups with the devices put into them. The actual values can be recalled from the device and updated back. For more information about the management of association groups, please refer to Chapters 4.4.2, 5.3.4 and 5.1.11.

Portable controllers without graphical interface allow managing association groups using special keys or key sequences. There is no general pattern how this is implemented in different remote controls.

4.3   Scenes

A scene refers to a desired status of a subset of devices in the home. Scenes are always connected to a desired situation in the home. Typical scene descriptions are:

- I am coming home.
- I am away.
- Having Dinner.
- Watching TV.

The user defines the desired status of different devices at one moment in a scene.

4.3.1   Examples

A scene *'I am away'* would define that the heating is in energy saving mode, all lights are turned off and the door is locked.

If and only if all devices in a scene can be treated similarly a scene can be realized with an association group. All devices in an association group will receive the very same command if the event happens that was defined as trigger for the association group.

The example above shows that association groups with similar commands to similar devices will not always meet the users requirements. Therefore, certain devices offer a more powerful way to handle the situations: **Scene Activation**.

These devices allow defining a list of devices with a certain well defined command that will be executed when the scene is activated.

Example: I am away

- Command 'Set(0)' to Ceiling Light 1
- Command 'Set(0)' to Ceiling Light 2
- Command 'Dim(50%)' to Outside Lamp
- Command 'Thermostat.Setback()' to Central Heating control
- Command 'Lock()' to Door Lock Front Door
- Command 'Lock()' to Door Lock Back Door

Similar to association groups, there are three requirements to be met:

- The actors need to be identified.
- The controller needs to be able to generate an event.
- The controller needs to know which actor to control in which way.

Compared to associations, the setup of a scene is more complicated because there are individual commands to be defined for each device that participates in the scene. Furthermore, there is much more data to be stored in a controller than for a simple association. This is the reason why only few devices support scenes compared to almost all sensors and controllers that support association groups. Figure 4.18 shows a scene execution.

Scenes are typically found in three different types of devices.

- Certain remote controls offer few extra scenes beside plenty of association groups. Typically, they have dedicated but-

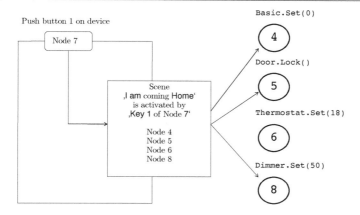

Figure 4.18: Scene execution

tons for scenes beside the standard control buttons for individual devices or groups of devices.

- There are dedicated scene controllers that are typically wall mountable or designed for desktops and capable of storing multiple scenes and execute them. Examples here are the scene wall controllers from Leviton or Cooper (both US devices).

- By far, the most popular way to define scenes is the web interface of the central controllers. The biggest advantage is a large user interface that gives a good overview. This makes the setup of scenes much easier. Besides, they have plenty of memory to store all scene-relevant data.

Normal buttons for association groups control have an ON and an OFF function to turn on or off the devices associated. Long press is typically used to execute dimming functions for dimmer connected. Scene controllers do not have an ON or OFF. The reason is that it is not trivial to deactivate a scene. This would mean that all devices need to go back to the status they had before the scene was activated. The scene controller would have to check the status of all the devices and store their value before executing the commands defined for the given scene activation. This would take too much time and effort so that no scene controller manufacturer has yet followed this path. Another option is to turn all devices back into a predefined status, e.g. **All Off**. This however can also be seen as a scene (a set of devices is turned into well-defined status) and it is handled exactly in this way.

Therefore, scene controllers only activate a scene but do not deactivate them anymore. Scene controllers that offer a deactivation button for a scene typically just turn off all devices connected to the very scene. Figure 4.3.1 shows the cooper scene controller as an example. Pushing a scene activation button executes the scene defined for this button and a blue LED turns on to indicate that this scene was executed last. It's possible to "turn off" the scene but only

Figure 4.19: In-Wall Scene Controller, manufactured by Cooper

by executing another scene or by hitting the same button again. In this case, all devices operated in the scene are turned off. Users need to make sure that only devices that can handle the OFF command (**Basic.Set(0)**) properly are operated by this scene.

4.3.2 Scene Snapshot

Most scene controllers allow to setup scenes wirelessly via Z-Wave using controllers or installation tools. If no graphical user interface is available for configuration some remote controls offer a nice tool: **Scene Snapshot**.

1. The first step is to assign all devices that shall be operated by a given scene to a single scene control button.
2. All these devices are now turned to the desired status. Cer-

tain light may go on, some may go off and dimmer may go to a certain dimming state.

3. A special command - e.g. a long press of the scene button - activates a process where the scene controller asks all devices for the status and stores this very status as scene.

Any press of the given scene activation button will now restore the same situation that was created and stored before. This is a very convenient way to setup a scene if there is no large screen interface for management.

4.3.3   Definition of scenes in central controllers

Thanks to their high computing power and storage capacity central controllers (IP gateways, Alarm Wall Panels, ...) are well suited to host definitions of scenes and execute them. Different manufacturers have implemented different ideas as to how to define scenes. However, a similar approach is to select a number of devices, define their desired status, and assign a certain a name to this setup. One single button will then allow issuing all necessary commands to set the selected devices into the desired state regardless of their previous state. Figure 4.20 shows an example of a definition dialog to create a scene. There are always three steps needed:

- Pick the devices that shall belong to a scene.
- Define the status of each device in this scene.
- Define a name for the scene and save the settings.

For the internal management scenes are not only referred to by name but by numerical **Scene-Ids** too. Using the command class `Central Scene` (explained later in this chapter) Z-Wave offers an explicit way to trigger scenes in central controllers. The `Central Scene` command class sends specific scene Ids that can be directly connected to the scenes already defined.

Figure 4.20: Scene setting in Z-Way Z-Wave Gateway (Source: Smart Home User Interface of Z-Way by z-wave.me)

4.3.4   Activation of scenes by timers

Central controllers offer an option to activate (trigger) scenes based on a timer. Most of the gateway hardware have an internal clock that can be used to trigger a scene without any further manual interaction. This is particularly useful for scenes that are frequently triggered or trigger always at the same time - e.g. in the morning.

The configuration options for timers differ from gateway to gateway, but there are some common ways to set timers:

- single time: on July 7th, 2012, 8:45
- periodical per day: every Friday morning 09:00
- frequently: every minute

Figure 4.21 shows the example of a user interface that allows to define timers.

4.3.5   Activation of scenes by wireless devices

There are a series of command classes designed to support the activation of scenes in a central controllers or IP gateway:

- **Scene Activation**: This command class allows to send a scene ID to a receiving device that is supposed to activate a scene identifies by this ID.
- **Scene Controller Configuration**: This command class is used to assign a certain scene ID to a certain association group. In most cases, all receivers of a command sent to an association group will receive a BASIC command. This is changed. The association group is now sending out a Scene Activation Command with the defined Scene ID and trigger a scene in the IP Gateway if this gateway is set into the association group.

  This command class is a simplified version of the much broader but complex command class *"Association Command Configuration Command Class."*
- **Scene Actuator Configuration**: With this command

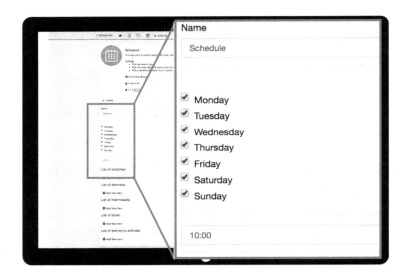

Figure 4.21: Example of a User Interface defining timers and schedules (Source: Smart Home User Interface of Z-Way by z-wave.me)

class, it is possible to assign a certain status of an actuator (switch, dimmer, etc.) to a scene ID. If this actuator receives a "Scene Activation Command" with this scene ID, the predefined status is activated (like "on", "off" or "50 percent dim" level).

This command class allows to store the information about a scene distributed in the actuators and not in a central place like an IP gateway. Unfortunately, only very few actuators support this function and as a consequence most scenes are stored and managed in the central IP Gateway.

- **Central Scene**: Since most networks are controlled by a central static controller or IP gateway the scenes get executed right there. The command class `Central Scene` reflects this. It essentially allows sending different numerical values to the controller that can be used to trigger scenes. Usually, controllers map these numbers to different keys. Besides the key press, the central scene also allows differentiating between "single click", "double click", "click and hold", etc.

This limits the scene handling to devices that explicitly support scene activation. Users however want to use all kind of devices to activate scenes, particularly wall controllers, remote controls and even sensors. Most of them were never designed for scene activation and therefore only support associations or sometimes not even this. This creates the challenge that the central controller

- receive a message from a device that was not designed for scene activation.
- They need to interpret them as scene commands.
- They need to distinguish different events from the same device in order to activate different scenes.

To accomplish this, central controllers use certain approaches to enable scene activation even for legacy devices that were not initially designed for scene activation.

Scene Activation

As described above certain Z-Wave controllers already explicitly support the activation of scenes (**Central Scene Command Class**). Their different buttons can be configured to send enumerated scene activation commands, which are received by the controller. Controllers with scene switching capability can be used for scene switching without further work and constrains by IP gateways.

Associations

Associations are used to establish switching relationship between a controlling and a controlled Z-Wave device. Typically, controlling devices send a **BASIC SET** command to perform a switching function in the controlled device.

If these **BASIC** switching commands are sent from a device to a central scene controller they can be interpreted as a scene switching command. The challenge is that the **BASIC SET** command does not allow sending any scene number information. Rather the **BASIC SET** command typically only supports the values 0x00 and 0xff. As long as the sending controller only has one push button or just one association group supported, a received **BASIC SET** command can be used to trigger to a scene easily.

If the sending controller device has more than one association group, the central scene controller is not able to differentiate between the different groups as they all send the very same **BASIC SET** command. The result is that certain buttons do not issue any command or all buttons will issue the very same command.

Multichannel Association

If the sending controller can send multichannel commands, it can be configured in a way to send different scene activation commands (still as BASIC SET or BASIC REPORT with values 0x00 or 0xff) to different channels, helping the intelligent "master" controller to distinguish different commands and activate different scenes accordingly. In order to use this "trick," the sending controller must support multichannel association.

Virtual Nodes

In some cases, the central scene controller is able to act as multiple virtual nodes in the network. It will then not only receive commands for one single Node-ID but for multiple Node-IDs. Associations can be set for each of these different Node-IDs that are all received by the same physical device. The central scene controller is now able to distinguish different commands and activate different scenes accordingly. In order to use this "trick," the hardware used for the central scene controller (USB stick plus software, set-top box, IP gateway) must support bridged devices. Only a handful of devices do this at the moment.

4.3.6   Activation of scenes by Boolean logic

Most scenes shall not only be triggered by a single event of a single condition but by a combination of different status information and events. For example, the night light will be turned on by a motion detector but only in the evening and not during the day. This means that different input variables need to be combined to generate the final scene-triggering event. The way this combination is achieved is called binary logic or Boolean logic. Explaining Boolean logic is not within the scope of this book. For more information, please refer to secondary literature such as [Tutorial2015] or [Givant2008].
Boolean logic has the three basic ways to combine variables:
- **AND**
- **OR**
- **NOT**

With these three elements, even complex relationships between variables can be described. In case of the evening light triggered by a motion detector, the definition looks quite simple:

IF (it is evening) **AND** (Motion detector triggers) $\to$ **THEN** (activate scene)

It is possible to connect more than two input variables using Boolean logic. However, some constrains need to be considered.

- The logical combinations, namely AND and OR always combine two variables. If more than two variables are combined, there is a need to set braces: The statement "A and B or C" has two meanings: (1) always A and then either B or C, (2) Either a combination of A and B or just C.
- There is a difference between status value and events. A scene can only be activated by one single event but this event can be combined with a list of status value. The scene is triggered only if the event happens and all the other status variables are in the desired status. In case a scene depends on two events than the trigger condition is only true if both events happen at the very same moment. This is quite unlikely.
  A combination of variables therefore always has one single event but a not limited list of other status values. Status values are 'after 17.00' (not right at 17.00 - this is an event), a certain switching state of a switch (not the change of the switching status - this is an event).

It is very difficult to create an intuitively usable and easy to understand user interface to create logical combination of variables. Certain gateway manufacturers have tried different approaches, but some vendors do not even offer these kinds of setup. Figure 4.22 shows a more or less successful graphical user interface for the definition of logical combinations and rules.

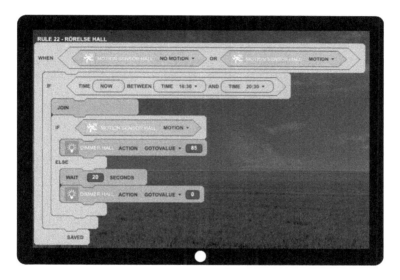

Figure 4.22: Example of a User Interface defining Boolean rules
and logic (Source: Zipato Tile User Interface by Zipato)

4.3.7   Complex Scenes with Scripting

Some complex settings are not even easy to describe with simple binary logic. Here programming or scripting is needed:

An example network has the following functions:

- An external rain sensor offers a status information that is either 1 (it is raining) or 0 (it is not raining).
- A window motor to turn **on** or **off** the roof window.
- A jalousie controller is opening or closing the window blind.

A script for this function may look like:

Listing 4.1: Pseudo Script Code to control a window

```
if rainsensor.status != 1:
        windowMotorControl.Set(0)
        // close the window
        while windowMotorControl.status != 0:
                sleep 1;
        jalousieController.Set(100)
else:
jalousieController.Set(0)
        while jalousieController.status != 0:
                sleep 1;
        windowMotorControl.Set(100)
        // close the window
```

The first and very obvious function is that the window is closed when it is raining and that the window is open when it is not raining. The window however should not be opened if the blind is closed because for some mechanical reasons the opening window will destroy the blind. The script thus waits for the blind to close until the status of the motor control indicates that the window is closed (status=0). In case it is not raining, the jalousie will open first and, only when the **jalousieController.status** indicates that the jalousie is open, the command for opening the window is issued.

Scripts in gateways allow defining and realizing very complex relationships and dependencies.

Points of discussion	association groups	Scenes
Easiness of setup	Very easy	More complicated
Switching by remote controls and wall controllers	Easy	May be complicated
Works, when IP gateway or Cloud Service is down	Yes	No
Activated by timers	Not possible	Possible
Mix of different switching status	Not possible	Possible
Activated by web interface	Not possible	Possible

Table 4.5: Comparison of scenes and associations

4.3.8   Comparison of association groups and Scenes

Both associations and scenes are suitable to control relationships between sensors, controllers and actors. They can be even mixed. However, it is recommended to stay with one concept to make the setup of the network easier.

Associations have one important advantage. They act decentrally. All scenes always need the gateway being involved and therefore acting as a single point of failure. Direct control of devices by sensors using associations is a decentral and therefore more robust way of controlling devices in smart homes.

Table 4.5 shows a comparison of scenes and associations with their pros and cons.

The net-net of this comparison is that associations are easier to use but limited in their functionality. Scenes may be more complicated but give users much more flexibility and power to define interdependencies and automation of the Z-Wave network.

4.4   User Interfaces

The user interface is the final building block to form a smart home control solution based on Z-Wave. There is no right or wrong way to create a user interface. User interfaces depend on style, local preferences, type, knowledge and skills of the people using it (... and yes, also the people creating it). It is also far beyond the scope of this book to describe the details of all user interfaces on the market in details. The Z-Wave standard defines very few aspects of the user interface leaving plenty of room for creativity on the manufacturers side.

However, some general guidelines seem to be similar across the different products and manufacturers choices:

4.4.1   Wall controllers and remote controls

Wall controllers and remote controls only have buttons to interact with LEDs or very small LCD panels to indicate statuses.

In case there is a LCD panel, setup, management and control is quite easy. In case there are only LEDs with one or with different colors, study of the device manual is usually required to decrypt the codes shown. A lot of wall controllers or remote control makers use

- red LEDs to indicate errors,
- green LEDs to indicate success,
- flashing LEDs to indicate the transmission of data,
- slow blinking LEDs to indicate that the device is in a certain state, e.g. ready for inclusion.

Figure 4.23 shows a remote control that has dedicated buttons for Inclusion, Exclusion, Learn Mode, and Association below a slideable cover plus four control buttons for scene control.

Figure 4.23: Dedicated buttons on a Z-Wave remote control (Source: Aeon Labs LLC)

4.4.2 Installer tools

Installer tools are special software tools that are used only during the installation and setup of the network. They typically don't provide a user interface for daily usage but very detailed technical data for professionals.

The following functions are mainly covered by installer tools.

1. Inclusion, Exclusion
2. Setting of Configuration Parameters as described in chapter 4.2.3
3. Management of Associations
4. Management of Routing

Associations can be set using very generic interfaces as seen in Figure 4.24.

4.4.3 Web-Interfaces for Users

Interfaces for users focus on three basic functions:

1. Visualization of Sensor Values
2. Direct control of actors
3. Activation of Scenes

Depending on the technology used and the display screen real estate these user interfaces can be quite simple or heavily ani-

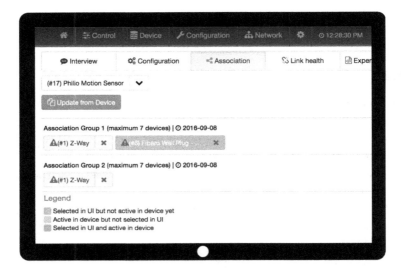

Figure 4.24: Setup for Association relationships (Source: Expert User Interface of Z-Way by z-wave.me)

Figure 4.25: Example of a smart home user interface on a mobile device

mated. Quite often the devices in the Z-Wave network can be placed on a floor plan or at least assigned to a certain room.

Figure 4.25 shows an example of a very basic Web user interface for smartphones or iPads that can be shown on typical hardware such as iPhone, Android, or Blackberry. Other interfaces may be more stylish but rarely provide substantially more functionality.

4.5   Wireless Security in Smart Homes

Security in the smart home is an important topic. Security concerns include the danger that the private home and the personal live is visible in the Internet for hackers but also for energy suppliers or other intelligence organization. People are also concerned that attackers may turn on or off their lights, manipulate their heating/cooling system or even unlock their door so that burglars can get into the house.

Security is also an important issue in information technology but the usual rules and technologies of Internet security and information technology can only be partly applied for the situation in the smart home. It is therefore worth to have a broader look on the topic.

4.5.1 General information about security and typical attacks

Security in information technology in general means the protection against three possible attacks:

- A third party gets access to private data.
- A third party can act on behalf of the attacked person.
- The information technology functions are made unavailable for the user, usually referred to as *Denial of Service*.

There are two common methods to protect data that is exchanged in public networks such as the Internet:

- Encryption of data.
- Authentication and Authorization.

Encryption protects data from being read by an unauthorized third party. Authorization and Authentication makes sure that no unauthorized person can obtain and use other peoples rights as users of a given service, e.g. a banking account.

Both mechanisms are designed for the transport of sensible and private data and the use of private and sensible services within the public unprotected Internet. The situation in a private smart home does not fully comply with this.

4.5.2 Encryption

The control of actions in the smart home only use small data packets compared to large packets with private content for data communication in information technology. The content of the data packets is even standardized and therefore there is not much to hide.

In some cases, encryption of these already known data does not provide any further security against attacks. A perfect example of this is the `Wakeup Notification Command` in Z-Wave (For details on this command and its use please refer to Chapter 3.3.2). Even if this communication would be perfectly encrypted, the information of this packet is not **in** the packet - it **is** the packet itself.

However, there may be data from sensors or other status information from other devices that can be of interest to attackers. That is why encryption of commands in the smart home is still needed, at least for a subset of the communication messages.

Encryption always needs encryption/decryption keys that must be available at both ends of the communication channel. This means that encryption has two points that can be attacked:

- Decrypt the message. Such an attack method, however, requires a fair amount of data to run statistical analysis. In smart homes with few and short packets, this seems almost impossible to do.
- Capture the encryption key. Key can be either distributed during production of the devices or they are exchanged later. In case of smart homes, a predefined key is only possible if all devices come from the same manufacturer. Having a preinstalled key is risky. If the key is leaked, all devices of all installations become vulnerable. The alternative is to exchange a network key during the pairing of the devices. This avoids having one single key for all networks but the key exchange itself may be vulnerable.

Both approaches for key exchange are used in contemporary smart home systems.

4.5.3   *Replay*-Attacks

The real practical thread to smart home security is that a hacker captures the packet and resends it at the wrong time. In case the attacker can refer the data packet to an interesting action in the house (like turning on a light or opening a door), this becomes either a dangerous or at least an annoying attack method. In such an attack, it is irrelevant whether or not the data were encrypted. An attack that captures a digital signal and retransmits it after some time is called **Replay Attack** and cannot be prevented by encryption alone.

The only way to protect a smart home from replay attacks is to use one-time keys that change with every transaction, also referred to as **Key Sequencing**. This approach is, among others, used for wireless car keys. Every time the key is used, it generates a new sequence key that follows certain protected patterns only known to the car itself. Even if such a wireless message is captured, it is quite worthless since it will never be accepted again. The security of the key sequence depends on the protection of the sequence algorithm that is programmed in both keys and car during production.

While this approach works perfectly fine for pre-manufactured pairs of devices, it will fail for dynamic networks with multiple communication partners from different manufacturers. The solution for this is known as one-time password.

The one-time password or one-time transaction key is referred to as **Nonce**. It is the same idea that is used to protect online banking transaction. Here, the Nonce is called TAN (transaction authorization number).

Using a TAN or a Nonce effectively protects data communication from replay attacks. However there are other ways to attack such a connection:

- The way Nonces are created is known. In this case the attacker can just create a new Nonce for his attack. This thread can be compared to having the TAN list of a bank account published.

- The *Nonce* is captured and does not reach the receiver. In this case, an attacker can use the Nonce within the timeout period to authorize a malfunctioning packet by claiming to be the authorized sender. This attack is also known as *Man-in-the-Middle* attack. A lot of attacks to online

Figure 4.26: Secure communication using nonces

banking use this method.

The use of Nonces together with an encryption of the whole packet is a very powerful protection against **Man-In-The-Middle** attacks. Additionally, the legitimate sender must be authenticated. The PIN/TAN solution is an implementation of this approach for online banking.

The best performance of Nonces is achieved if they are not dependent on each other at all but can be randomly generated every time they are used. This provides very good protection of the communication, but it also creates the need to transport the Nonce, generated by the receiver, to the transmitter. It is possible to transport the Nonce the same way the real data is transported if and only if the communication is sufficiently encrypted. Since the Nonce is only transported one time, there is no chance for a *Replay* attack. The encryption does not even have to be too strong. It is sufficient to delay the possible use of the Nonce by the attacker to the moment the legal transmitter has used it. Hereafter, the Nonce is invalid and useless.

4.5.4   *Denial-of-Service-Attack*

Another well-known attack method is the so-called **Denial-of-Service** attack. Here, the goal of the attacker is not to get access to private data or act on behalf of an attacked person, but to suppress any successful communication. Denial-of-Service is a destructive attack method.

In wireless communication, it is impossible to have 100 % protection against *Denial-of-Service* attacks. An attacker can always build a broadband transmitter and jam all wireless communication. This is true for all wireless control in the smart home, hence for cellphone and Wi-Fi traffic too.

The higher protection against Denial-of-Service is an often-cited argument for wired communication in a smart home. The argument is valid but incomplete since mobile phones and Wi-Fi Internet are still used in these smart homes. At least these wireless communication methods remain vulnerable to denial of service.

It is equally easy to build a *Denial-of-Service* attack method for Wi-Fi or cellphone, but the fun and the benefit for the attacker is limited. It is neither possible to perform any public event (such as turning off all lights on a certain street), nor does it provide any tangible advantage like getting into a home. There are easier, cheaper, and better methods to annoy people than jam their wireless connection. Every window smashed by stone has a higher impact, particularly in wintertime.

4.5.5   Further aspects of wireless security

Another inherent protection against *Denial-of-Service* and *Man-in-The-Middle* is the limitation of wireless range. Z-Wave as an example does not even use the maximum allowed transmitting power of 25 mW but sends out signals with few mW only. The wireless range outside the house is therefore limited to maximum

100 m or typically 40 m. Alternative technologies in the same frequency band may reach wireless ranges of up to 1300 m. The lower wireless range of Z-Wave is compensated by the capability to use devices as routers. A high transmitting power of a wireless technology increases the vulnerability to attacks. In case the signal does not go far beyond the own home, an attacker needs to be in proximity to the home to perform any attack.

Finally, an important part of the security discussion in wireless networks is the cost/benefit ratio. The often-cited foreign hacker that gets access to the energy consumption data of a washing machine on a western household is simple not a very meaningful scenario. A hacker, 1000 km away does not have any tangible benefit from hacking into the infrastructure of a stranger. He will invest his criminal energy in more profitable projects like hacking the same persons bank account. Being in front of a home gives more options for attack but even here a stone is cheaper and easier to get than a complicated jamming electronics, not even mentioning the fact that the knowledge about how to throw a stone is easier to obtain than the knowledge how to build a jamming transmitter.

Even the danger that an attacker may electronically unlock the door becomes mitigated considering that a trained burglar takes less than five seconds to break the contemporary mechanical door lock.

4.5.6 The conventional security concept of Z-Wave

The security architecture of Z-Wave has evolved over time. Initially, Z-Wave—like most other wireless technologies at the beginning of the new millennium—just had a simple line encoding that was, meanwhile, fairly easy to decode having modern technologies on hand. Additionally, the usually unknown Home-ID of the network to be attacked was another hurdle to quickly break into an existing Z-Wave network. Nevertheless, simple read and reply attacks where demonstrated successfully using off-the-shelf mi-

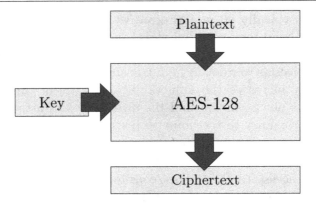

Figure 4.27: Encryption using AES128

crocontroller hardware [Fouladi2013] and a quite expensive Software Defined Radio (SDR) [Hall2016].

In 2009, mainly driven by the new popular door locks, a new security architecture **Security Command Class V1** was introduced. This command class adds two important features:

- Standard Z-Wave packets can be encapsulated into a secure container as shown in Figure 4.28. This container extends the rather small Z-Wave command to a minimum encryptable block length of multiples of 128 bit and encrypts them using the industry-standard encryption method AES 128. The Advanced Encryption Standard (AES), also known by its original name Rijndael, is a specification for the encryption of electronic data established by the U.S. National Institute of Standards and Technology (NIST) in 2001 [Nsa2003],[Aes2001].

  AES has been adopted by the U.S. government and is now used worldwide. The algorithm described by AES is a symmetric-key algorithm, meaning the same key is used for both encrypting and decrypting the data. In AES128 this key has a length of 128 bit or 7 Byte.

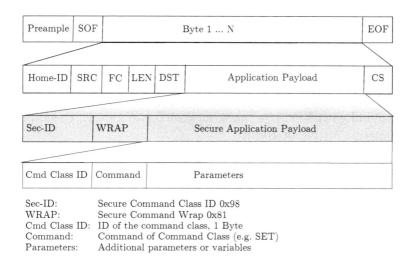

Sec-ID: Secure Command Class ID 0x98
WRAP: Secure Command Wrap 0x81
Cmd Class ID: ID of the command class, 1 Byte
Command: Command of Command Class (e.g. SET)
Parameters: Additional parameters or variables

Figure 4.28: Security Command Class V1 Encapsulation

- Every communication wrapped by the **Security Command Class V1** is protected by a single Nonce (one time password). This ensures that no packet is accepted twice as described in chapter 4.5.3.

The introduction of the **Security Command Class V1** provided a reasonably well working protection of wireless communication. Not even the more sophisticated hacking attack described in [Hall2016] was able to break into a connection protected by the command class.

However the **Security Command Class V1** implementation has two major disadvantages:

Communication and Processing overhead

In Z-Wave the encryption of data messages is done in hardware.
The Z-Wave transceiver has an AES encryption core embedded.
Therefore, encryption will not introduce any further delay and
only minimal extra power consumption. The real cost is latency.
Here are some estimations:

According to Table 3.2, the transmission of a normal Z-Wave
command with 40 kbit/s takes between 5 and 15 ms. To simplify,
we assume a time of 10 ms.

To turn on a switch within the Z-Wave security architecture, the
following data needs to be exchanged (see Figure 4.26):

1. Request for a Nonce (from sender to receiver)
2. Confirmation of the Nonce request (from receiver to sender)
3. Transmission of the Nonce (from receiver to sender)
4. Confirmation of the Nonce (from sender to receiver)
5. Transmission of the command, encrypted with the Nonce
   (from sender to receiver)
6. Conformation of the command (from receiver to sender)

This shows that the communication effort triples when using a
secure environment. Using the 10 ms time delay this means in
total a 60 ms execution time for the whole transaction. After the
transaction, the sensor has to stay inactive for a while because
of the duty cycle regulation mentioned in chapter 2.2.

For a simple switching command, this is quite acceptable. Assuming a scene is triggered with five or even more lights to switch
user will experience the delay of up to one second. In case the
packet is routed, the delay is even longer.

Initial exchange of network key

As mentioned above all communication in AES 128 is encrypted
and decrypted using the very same key - called the network key.
This key is a random 128-bit value that needs to be exchanged
between all members of the network. Having a preset key for all

secure devices is too risky as one can see in the example of the leaked key of the Philips Lighting System Hue [Markoffnov2016]. A prefabricated key is also not a good choice for an open multivendor system such as Z-Wave. Hence the network code needs to be exchanged between Z-Wave devices over the air. This is usually done right after inclusion of a new device that needs to communicate secure. The exchange of the key itself is encrypted as well but the key for this encrypted packet is preset and therefore known (its 7 times 0x00). The already known first key can be used to decode the packet with the real key. This is done by any new device joining the network and hence it can be done by any attacker eavesdropping the network at the moment of inclusion. Once the key is exchanged its practically impossible to break into a secure communication of Z-Wave.

Consequences

While the initial key exchange was and is a manageable problem, the communication overhead is a real challenge since it does not only delay the execution of communication but also consumes three times the battery power compared to non-secure communication.

Manufacturers and users need to balance the need for security with the desire for convenience and fast reaction of the electrical installation. The Z-Wave standard did not enforce the use of **Security Command Class V1** for non-security related communication relations but makes it mandatory for security-related devices such as door locks only.

4.5.7   The security architecture S2

In 2016 a complete new security architecture was introduced; **Security Command Class V2**, in short **S2**. It fixes the problems mentioned above and adds some very strong additional functions. The new S2 security system of Z-Way sets the standard in smart homes and will serve as benchmark for all other security systems to be introduced in the future.

Encryption

The AES128 remains the block encryption technology of choice. It is standardized, accepted for highly classified government and military communication as well as for financial transactions. There is a wealth of scientific work proofing that the encryption is still the right choice to protect valuable data.

Device Specific Key - DSK

In the security architecture S2 every device has an own individual device specific key in its memory. This key is called Device Specific Key or DSK. It is generated randomly during production of the device and it will be used to identify the device during the establishment of secure communication channel.

The key has a length of 16 byte and is usually printed on the device in 8 groups of decimal values. Beside the numerical representation of the DSK there is a QR code that simplifies the capture of the DSK if needed. In case the DSK must be typed into a form only the first group of numbers will be used. This digit group is called PIN code and shall be printed in bold and underlined. Figure 4.29 shows a typical QR code of the DSK and its numerical representation as printed on a product label.

Secure Network Key Exchange

The Security Architecture S2 still knows network keys that need to be exchanged right after inclusion. S2, however, now protects this key exchange using a technology called "Diffi–Hellman." The Diffi–Hellman key exchange is a specific method of securely exchanging cryptographic keys over a public channel and was named after the scientists Whitfield Diffie and Martin Hellman.

zws2dsk:34028-23669-20938-46346-33746-07431-56821-14553

Figure 4.29: Z-Wave S2: QR code example

They had published the scheme in 1976 [Diffie1976]. Diffi–Hellman exchanges a shared secret—the network key over an unsecure communication medium—the air.

Figure 4.30 explains the idea. Both communication partners start with a preset value—here the "common ground." Each of the communication partner has an internal secret that is not shared with anybody (the secret ingredients). They now mix the common ground with their individual secret. Here it is important that this transaction is a one-way-transaction easy to do in one way but hard to do the reverse way. For the cryptographic Diffi–Hellman–Algorithm, this operation is a the modulo p [2] of the multiplication of two numbers, the known original plus the secret. Only knowing the modulo makes it impossible to conclude on the original variables if and only if the modulo p is big enough. Both sides now exchange the mix to each other and both side mix

---

[2]In computing, the modulo operation finds the remainder after division of one number by another - sometimes called modulus. The current implementation of Diffi–Hellmann in Z-Wave does not use a simple modulo but applies the more effective elliptic curve as best known way to make this calculation secure [Edhc2013].

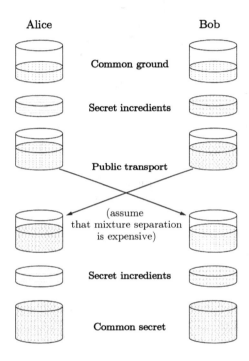

Figure 4.30: The principle of Diffi-Hellman Key Exchange (Source: A.J. Han Vinck, University of Duisburg-Essen)

the received mix again with their own secret. The result is on both sides the very same shared secret key because of the original Id mixed by secret one mixed by secret two. No third party that can eavesdrop one of the two exchanged values is able to construct the same shared secret key since it lacks the secrets that remain inside the communication partners. Again, this is only true if it is not possible to reverse the operation that generated the mix exchanged in public.

All initial key exchanges in Z-Wave S2 apply Diffi–Hellman and hence it is not possible to leak a network key while the key of a network remains unique for this network. This means that there is only one theoretical option to leak the key—get in physical possession of a device and try to read the key out of the embedded memory of the ASIC. Needless to say, this is very difficult but in theory not impossible.

Z-Wave S2 has thus added one more layer of security. It allows segmenting the network in different domains each having its own network key. This allows keeping sensitive devices such as door locks in one group while having others more vulnerable devices, e.g. an outdoor switching plug that can be stolen - in a different group.

Nonce Handling

The communication overhead in the `Security Command Class V1` is caused by the application and delivery of a Nonce prior to any real communication. S2 solves this problem too. It now uses so called **SPAN** (Singlecast Pre-Agreed Nonce) tables.

Both communication partners pre-establish a list of Nonces that are used during communication. When there is a need to generate more Nonces, this information can be exchanged beforehand piggybacking on normal communication and not causing any additional traffic. Of course, an algorithm needs to ensure that both table contents are in sync and wrong Nonces are detected.

Compared to the exchange of nonces right before communication, the use of SPAN tables has one disadvantage. The validity of the SPAN table entries is no longer limited by a timeout or a synchronized clock. Therefore, it is possible to perform a delay attack by intercepting an encrypted message while at the same time jamming the intended receiver. This way, the receiver SPAN is not incremented and the receiver will accept the encrypted message when an attacker decides to transmit the delayed message. This attack further requires that the attacker returns a MAC layer acknowledgement to the sender to avoid that the user gets error messages (For more information about the MAC layer acknowledgement please refer to Chapter 3.1.6).

This sounds like a theoretical attack. Nevertheless, Z-Wave S2 has tools to protect communication against this case: A new Command Class `Supervision` can be used for S2 delivery acknowledgement. Only the intended receiver can respond correctly to a `Supervision.Get()` command.

The reduction in security using SPAN samples is only theoretical in nature. The savings of communication overhead resulting in shorter answering times for commands and lower usage of battery power, however, are the tangible benefits of this approach.

Authentication

One challenge in security is the protection of the communication. The other challenge is authentication. Authentication makes sure that the communication peer is indeed the communication peer it pretends. In the offline world, this is achieved in most cases using a passport or national ID card. This passport shows the picture of the owner together with the name and therefore border officers can check for the name instead of scanning a database of pictures to find people that are allowed (or not) to enter the country.

Traditionally, Z-Wave applies a simple but effective form of authentication. When a controller tries to include a device, the user

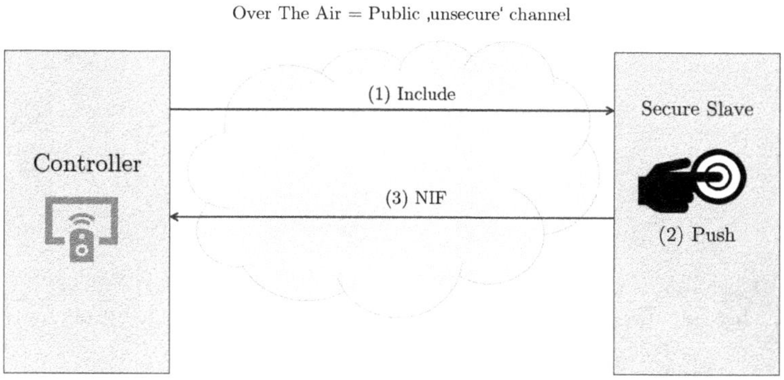

Over The Air = Public ‚unsecure' channel

Figure 4.31: Z-Wave Classic: Authentication by push a button on the device

must perform an action on this very device (pushing a button, powering, etc.). This ensures that this device in hand is the device that will appear on the user interface of the controller right after inclusion. Figure 4.31 shows this process.

In Z-Wave S2, this classic way is called **Authentication S0**. All devices using this way to authenticate share the same network key.

The security architecture S2 introduces three more network keys that are exchanged between the controller and devices that meet certain authentication requirements:

- **S0** - the legacy way to authenticate
- **S2 Unauthenticated**
- **S2 Authenticated**
- **S2 Access Control**

During the inclusion a new device supporting S2 will request a list of network keys depending on their authentication options. Figure 4.32 shows a user interface of a controller displaying the network key requests.

The network key **S2 Unauthenticated** is received if a device

Figure 4.32: Z-Wave S2: Request of different network keys by a new device (Source: Expert User Interface of Z-Way by z-wave.me)

does not require a special authentication. Certain controllers may display the DSK transmitted during the inclusion and the user can verify this key with the key printed on the device. However devices only requesting **S2 Unauthenticated** may not even show its DSK. In this case communication using the network key **S2 Unauthenticated** will not provide any higher level of security than S0.

The two other network keys require an authentication of the device. Authentication means here that the user is required to actively verify the identity of a device, e.g. by typing in a DSK or scanning the DSK from a QR code.

During inclusion a device with support for **S2 Authenticated** will only provide an incomplete DSK the user has to complete. The completed SDK will then be verified with the key of the device to proof that the DSK was read correctly. Since the DSK or at least the first 5 digits - the so called PIN code - where identified manually this can be compared to a *two-factor authentication* where a secret is exchanged on a second communication channel beside the wireless communication - here the QR code or the human eye.

Figure 4.33 shows this process. This protects against the very unusual and possible attack to highjack a communication by replacing the identity of included device with a manipulated one.

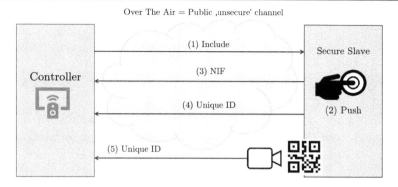

Figure 4.33: Z-Wave S2: Authenticated Access

The highest level of authorization in S2 is called **S2 Access Control**. Technically it follows the same process like **S2 Authenticated** but it maintains another network key. This reflects the special sensitivity of access devices such as door locks.

Assuming there is a device with support for **S2 Authenticated** but this device is placed outside the home - e.g. a outdoor siren. In theory it could be possible to steal this device and reverse engineer the internal network key.

Agreed - this is a very theoretical case but it shows how far the new Z-Wave security architecture S2 goes.

It is possible that the very device supports multiple authentication methods. In this case its up to the user and/or up to the controller to decide which network keys will be granted. If S0 or S2 Unauthenticated are requested most of the controllers will just grant them to the device, which the request for **S2 Authenticated** or **S2 Access Control** requires manual interaction.

Figure 4.34 shows a user interface asking for a PIN code and Figure 4.35 shows the list of devices in the network with their network key granted. In this example only devices number 11 and 12 support S2 and device number 11 failed during authen-

Verify device PIN

Verify PIN code for new device

11 s remain

PIN 0   · 1421   · 53837   · 52362   · 28824   · 51434   · 46734   · 24069

× Cancel   ✓ confirm

Figure 4.34: Z-Wave S2: Request for pin code for S2 Authenticated Access (Source: Expert User Interface of Z-Way by z-wave.me)

Figure 4.35: Z-Wave S2: List of devices with network keys granted (Source: Expert User Interface of Z-Way by z-wave.me)

tication while device number 12 the network keys **S0** and **S2 Unauthenticated** where granted.

Consequences

The Z-Wave S2 security architecture addresses all common challenges of smart home security and fixes all problems of the classical Z-Wave security `Security Command Class V1`. It does no longer, even in theory, enables eavesdropping on the network key during inclusion and does not introduce additional communication overhead for Nonce exchange. This is the reason that the Z-Wave Alliance decided to make Z-Wave S2 mandatory for all new devices certified after April 2, 2017 [Sigma2017]. Legacy devices based on Z-Wave Plus can be upgraded via "Over the Air" (OTA) firmware update.

Z-Wave S2 is certainly the most advanced security architecture in the whole smart home world. They key thesis for security and S2 is as follows:

- The main thread for smart homes are *Replay-* and *Denial-of-Service-* attacks.
- Encryption does not protect against these typical ways of attack but still provides protection against sensor and status eavesdropping
- Real protection against replay attacks is only possible using single-time key codes, called Nonces.
- Security requires that all Nonces are generated independent of each other. This implies additional communication overhead but gives a very high level of security.
- Wireless Meshing and lowered transmission power limit the range of the wireless network and increases the cost and risk for a denial-of-service attack.
- There is no 100 % technical protection against *Denial-of-Service* attacks.
- Z-Wave S2 does not only provide best in class encryption using AES 128 but also best in class network key exchange using Diffi-Hellmann algorithm.
- Z-Wave S2 protects against replay-attacks using nonces. Thanks to SPAN tables there is no communication overhead.
- Z-Wave S2 introduces different level of authorization reflecting different application types and devices. This also results in different security domains using different network keys.

Chapter 5

Z-Wave in action - Tips and Tricks

This chapter will provide some useful and practical tips how to build, manage and use a Z-Wave network.

5.1 Building the network - general workflow

Every Z-Wave network is built following the same steps:

1. Define the desired functions.
2. Pick the right devices.
3. Include all devices into one network.
4. Configure the devices according to the user's need.
5. Set all association and define all scenes.
6. Do some final housekeeping work.

5.1.1 Defining the desired functions

A smart home can have plenty of functions and the planning process can be overwhelming. It makes sense to clearly define the high-level services first. These services should be broken down by rooms or floors and by the basic functions of an intelligent home network:

- light,
- heating,
- climate,
- security,
- safety,
- door lock,
- media and entertainment,
- energy management,
- windows.

This is a high-level list with items that may overlap with each other. For example, having a window open-close control is both a security feature and a climate control feature.

A second step is to define where the smart home will be controlled from:

- Wall controllers - where placed?
- Remote controls - how many?
- Smart Phone.
- Web Browser.
- Wall panel.

The third step of planning is to create a list of all rooms or floors and assign what functions shall be available in what rooms. There may be functions that are applied to all rooms and functions that only apply to the whole home as such. Such a list might look like this:

- Sleeping room: safety (smoke), light, window control
- Kitchen: light, heating, safety (smoke + water leakage), window control
- Living room: light, heating, media
- All rooms: energy management
- House: main door control, back door control

A few advantages of Z-Wave are that it

- can be used to retrofit existing homes and
- can be applied step by step over time.

If the planning of a whole home looks too big, expensive, or complicated, it is no problem to start with a very small network focusing on one or two applications. Typically, small and single-focus networks may solve problems like:

- Only managing the main door to avoid phone calls like "I forgot my key".
- Just combining a second wall switch beside the bed to avoid the typical way to get into the bedroom: turn on ceiling light $\to$ walk to bed $\to$ turn on bed light $\to$ walk back to door $\to$ turn off the ceiling light $\to$ walk back to bed $\to$ go to bed $\to$ turn off the bed light.
- Installing a central energy meter to get an idea when the most energy is consumed.
- Being able to turn off all big standby-power consumers such as computers, TV, Hi-Fi etc. when leaving the home.
- Being able to turn up the heat while being on the way home.

These solutions can be easily expanded step by step. This is one of the big advantages of wireless technologies in general and Z-Wave in particular.

5.1.2   Picking the right devices

The selection of the devices is a complex task, because multiple aspects need to be taken into consideration:

- Light control:
  - What kind (color, shape) of wall control elements are suitable?
  - Shall light be switched or dimmed?
  - What kind of lighting elements are installed (traditional light, high voltage halogen, low voltage halogen,

LED, CFL)?

- What kind of power wiring system is available in the house (2 wire or 3 wire cabling)?
- How many lights are there per room? Are they wired, like ceiling or wall lamps, or do they stand alone, like a floor light?

- Heating:
  - What kind of heating system is already installed or planned and how it is going to be controlled (central boiler, floor heating with central control, floor heating with zones, radio thermostats, mains controlled HVAC,...)?
  - Shall the heating be controlled in the room with local elements?
  - Is heating and cooling combined?

- Doors:
  - What kind of doors are used (thickness, locking system, dimension of door)?
  - Shall there be handles on the outside, are the doors left/right winged?
  - Which colors and finishes will match the design of the doors best?

- Windows:
  - Shall the windows just be monitored or also moved?
  - Roof windows or standard windows?
  - What kind of jalousie controller shall be installed?

- Energy Management:
  - What devices beyond lighting and heating shall be monitored (Dish Washer, washing machine, freezer, fridge, sauna, computer)?

This book does not intend to give correct product recommendations but to list down the right questions. There are well-organized online shops and home automation professionals available for help in picking the devices and calculating the costs.

Links to major sites can be found in the Annex A.

> Here are some more technical Z-Wave related constrains for device picking:
> - If there is at least one battery-operated sensor or actor (FLiRS devices are ok), there must be a static controller like an IP gateway or a wall panel.
> - If devices shall be controlled from a web browser or a Smartphone, an IP gateway is a must too.
> - Battery-operated devices cannot route for other devices. If a network only consists of battery-operated devices, there is no routing and the wireless coverage is limited. Its recommended to have a fair distribution of mains powered devices to maintain network functions and network stability.

5.1.3   Z-Wave Wall Switches versus Wall Inserts

Different countries have different ways to wire wall switches. This ranges from quite large wall boxes in North America or Italy over the commonly used 60 mm diameter box for Central Europe down to the very tiny 40 m boxes popular in Denmark.

The strategy to deal with wall installations is determined by two factors:

1. The size of the wall box.
2. The variety of different designs for wall switches, usually driven by the variety of wall switch makers.

In North America (Lutron, Leviton, Cooper, Jasco, ...), in United Kingdom (MK, Honeywell) or in Italy (Btcino) installers typically choose to replace the whole switch by a new smart switch or smart dimmer. Figure 5.1 shows such a device.

Countries with a broader variety of wall switch designs like most

Figure 5.1: North American smart wall switch (Source: Jasco)

of the other European countries or most Asian countries have to choose between two approaches:

1. Replace the existing wall switch by a new product with wireless capabilities if there is a reasonable design available.

2. Keep the conventional analog switch in place but put a so-called wireless **switching insert** behind the old switch. The switch itself will then no longer directly control the mains power but sends a control signal to the insert only. This insert will then control the mains power depending on wireless signals or the position of the conventional switch. Figure 5.2 shows the schematic.

Wall Inserts are installed inside the wall box behind the conventional switch.

Wall Switches comply with the IEC norm with a depth of max 28 mm. They will therefore fit into every 45 or 65 mm deep box and can even be mounted into 35 mm deep boxes.

Even the smallest Z-Wave switching inserts are 16 mm high. That is why they can only be placed in 65 mm deep boxes. Application in 45 mm boxes is possible in theory but requires perfect cables and a lot of effort.

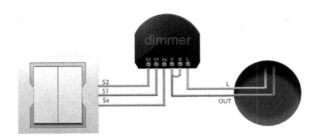

Figure 5.2: Schematics of Wall Insert installation

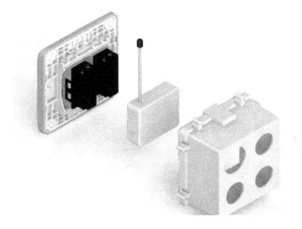

Figure 5.3: Wall Insert in wall box behind conventional wall switch

The intuitive operation of dimmers and blind controls is similar to the window lifter in cars. There is a neutral position without any action. A short click on the upper or lower part of the paddle moves the motor in one of the end positions respective turns the dimmer entirely on or off. Keeping the paddle pushed allows positioning the motor on the desired position between the end points resp. set the dimmer to a desired level by releasing the paddle.

Complete Z-Wave wall switches implement the control functions in the very same way. Wall inserts however use the switching paddles of the conventional wall switch. Typically, they only offer two control paddle positions. Due to the lack of a neutral position they are used in a "toogle" mode. Every switch into the ON-position results in the change of the switching state (on after off respective OFF after ON). Keeping the switch in the ON-position emulates the "click and hold" function to dim a light or to position a motor. This allows dimming and setting the motor but is a very unexpected function of a wall switch. Guests and other family members may not appreciate this strange way to operate a wall switch.

Therefore, most switching inserts simply accept the position of the switch as switching control state of the insert. The paddle in ON position will result in switching the load on and the paddle in OFF-Position will turn the load off. This mode realizes the intuitively expected behavior of a wall switch but does not allow to dim the dimmer into any dimming level except full on and full off and to set a controlled motor into any other position than the end position.

Furthermore, a switching status change caused by a wireless command may contradict with the paddle position of the locally controlling conventional switch, a situation known from the so-called hotel circuit where two switches can simultaneously control one single light only.

Wall inserts however have one big advantage over wireless wall switches. The design of the wall element remains unchanged. Wall switches are available in a series of different designs but conventional switches are available in many more design versions. In case there is no design available that is identical or similar to the rest of the installation, a wall insert may be the only option to keep identical wall element design while enjoying the advantage of wirelessly controlled smart home functions.

All these facts result in some simple guidelines for installation of switches in countries with constraints on the size and variety of wall switch designs. Choose wireless wall switches if

1. you have 35 or 45 mm deep wall boxes **OR**
2. you do a complete new installation of all wall elements **OR**
3. there is a wall switch that looks similar to your existing design.

Choose wall inserts if

1. you have 65 mm wall boxes **AND**
2. you already have installed wall switches in a certain design **AND**
3. there is no wall switch available that matches your wall switch design.

5.1.4 Including everything into a single network

Unless there are special requirements or super large networks, all devices will be included in one single wireless network. A Z-Wave network can manage up to 232 devices. However, a typical number of nodes in a fully equipped home is in the range of 50–80. This means there is plenty of room for future expansion and enhancements.

A Z-Wave network is built by a controller. There is always one single primary controller that is responsible for the network. In case there is a central controller available, this central controller should be picked as the main controller simply because the user interface is very convenient and the central controller offers backup and restores functions in case something goes wrong.

If there is no central controller, any other controller can act as a primary controller and the role of the primary controller can also be handed over to a different controller when desired.

For the setup and the configuration of a network, it may even be desirable to have different controllers to do the work. All inclusions can be done with a remote control as primary controller and the role of the primary controller is then handed over to a central controller for further operations. However, the central controller may have to reconfigure all devices to make sure the wakeup interval and the notification target node (mailbox) are set correctly and all information generated during the device interview is available.

It is also possible to do it the other way around. A central controller of software may be very beneficial for the setup work even if the network is later only operated by wall controllers and remote controls. The software then acts as an installer tool just for setup and configuration.

5.1.5   Way to include devices

The basic process of inclusion is described in chapter 3.1.3.

- The controller is turned into an inclusion mode.
- The new device is in factory default. It was not included into a different network or it was reset.
- Depending on the different methods of inclusion this inclusion needs to be confirmed on the device:
  1. With the so-called **network wide inclusion** the device can be included being in every position in the home as long as there is at least one Z-Wave device of this network in wireless range.
  2. The **standard inclusion** requires to have the new device in wireless range of the including controller.
  3. The almost obsolete **Low Power-Inclusion** requires

the device to be in direct proximity (up to 50 cm) of the including controller.

- The most convenient way is the so-called **auto-inclusion**. The device is just powered up to confirm inclusion. Typically, a device remains about 30 seconds in the auto-inclusion mode and will confirm any inclusion attempt by a controller during this time if the device was not yet included before. Auto-inclusion can be done as standard inclusion or network-wide inclusion.
- Technically the new device needs to send out a *Node Information Frame* to confirm inclusion.

When Z-Wave was developed in the early 2000 years, security considerations have driven the decision for the inclusion mode and a high hurdle for inclusion—the low power inclusion mode - was established.

After gaining more experience in the field the developers have realized that end users appreciate convenience more than a very high level of security. The first step was the standard inclusion, followed by the network wide inclusion and finally the auto inclusion function was added. However, even in the auto inclusion function the user needs to be in physical possession of the device to complete the process. Even in case that he wants to include a device, but at the same time a neighbor was just a blink of a second earlier and "got" the device, he is still able to exclude the device and repeat the process until his own controller included the new device successfully. Chapter 4.5.7 explains the new options Security S2 adds to authenticating devices.

Wall controllers or remote controls typically have either dedicated buttons for inclusion (as shown in Figure 5.4) or they use a special key sequence to turn the controller into the inclusion mode.

The inclusion mode is indicated by a blinking LED or by any other reasonable way. The inclusion mode typically times out if no inclusion takes place. If the controller was successfully including a device, it will either terminate the inclusion mode or

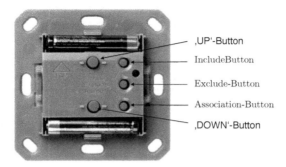

Figure 5.4: Wall controller with special button for inclusion (Source: Duewi Handelsgesellschaft)

continue with the inclusion until the mode times out or a special button terminates the inclusion mode. The behavior depends on the manufacturers implementation. Please refer to the manual of the controller for further details.

Central controllers, IP gateways or Z-Wave control software solutions follow the same process. They offer virtual buttons for inclusion and for exclusion and will indicate when the inclusion mode is active and when it was terminated. Figure 5.5 shows an example of a user interface of a Z-Wave software indicating that it is in active inclusion mode.

As mentioned before the new device needs to confirm the inclusion right on the device. Different ways are possible:

- Initial powering of the device confirms inclusion if this very device supports the Auto-Inclusion function.
- Single click on a button of the device, e.g. the rocker.
- Triple Click of a button within a defined time. This time depends on the vendor and may be between 1 and 3 seconds.
- Keep a button pushed for some time.

Z-Wave does not specify the way an inclusion is to be confirmed. It is only mandatory **that** an inclusion of the device is possible

Figure 5.5: Example of inclusion function in central controllers web interface (Source: Expert User Interface of Z-Way by z-wave.me)

and that the process to do this is described in the manual.

The auto inclusion and the single or triple click are a common way to confirm inclusion of a device. Nevertheless, manufacturers are creative to find new and unexpected ways for the inclusion process. Therefore, Z-Wave Plus—for information on Z-Wave Plus, please refer to Chapter 1.6.4—has further limited the possible options to include a device.

There are a couple of reasons why an inclusion can fail. **By far the most frequent reason is that the device to be included was already included in a different network.** The simple fix of this problem is to use the exclusion function of the controller to exclude the device first before it gets included again. Exclusion can be done by any controller not only the controller that was used for inclusion.

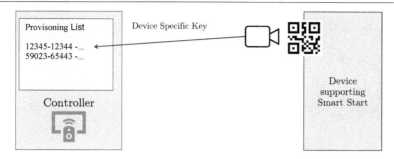

Figure 5.6: Smart Start: Scanning QR code

5.1.6 Smart Start

The introduction of the new security layer S2 as described in Chapter 4.5.7 allows significantly improving and simplifying the inclusion process. This new inclusion process is called **Smart Start**.

Technically Smart Start reverses the process a new device is included by a controller. Before Smart Start the controller had to be turned into the so called inclusion mode looking for new devices to be included.

In Smart Start the controller is always able to include new devices when they announce themself. New devices supporting Smart Start will announce their interest to be included right after being powered up. To make sure only the right controller includes the right device the S2 device specific key is used. This key must be captured by the controller prior to the inclusion attempt and stored in a so called **provisioning list** inside the controller. This provisioning list can be filled in three different ways:

- The user scans the QR code of the new device prior to powering it up.
- The user types-in the DSK into a form provided by the Uer Interface of the controller. Figure 5.8 shows a user interface

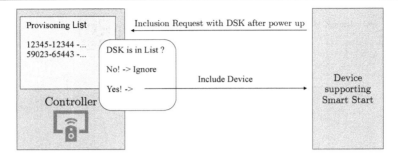

Figure 5.7: Smart Start: Checking Inclusion Request

as example.

• The reseller or installer scans the QR codes before shipping the devices. The full list is then transferred to the controller.

Figure 5.6 shows this process using the QR code. When QR is not readable the full DSK must be inserted into the provisioning list. Compared to the S2 Authentication it is not sufficient just to type-in the 5 digit pin code.

Once the controller received an inclusion request by a new device it will check if the DSK of this device is in its provisioning list. Only in this case the controller will include the new device. Other inclusion requests are simply ignored. Figure 5.7 shows this process that runs automatically right after powering on the device.

Smart Start has quite a few advantages:

• It unifies the way a new device is included. It is not longer necessary to know the specific inclusion action on the device (such as tripple click a button, click the button behind cover, ...).

• It allows to "pre-pair" devices to eliminate any inclusion action at the customers site. Installers and distributors wil just scan the QR codes of the devices delivered to one site.

Figure 5.8: Smart Start: User Interface for DSK (Device Key)

The list of the QR code contents, means the provisioning list, will be sent to the controller and the rest is magic. Once the devices are plugged in the will just work out of the box.

- All devices are authenticated.

5.1.7 Inclusion of Controllers

From the user point of view the inclusion of a controller by another controller looks like a normal inclusion of a device by the controller. However, behind the scenes more information needs to be exchanged to get the new controller "up to speed" to be able to act as a secondary controller in the network. All the network information of the primary controller needs to be copied to the new secondary controller. Therefore, a controller inclusion is sometimes also referred to as controller replication. Figure 5.9 shows the process on the network level.

A controller is able to include a device as a primary controller or inclusion controller but at the same time the device can be included by a different controller as secondary controller in his network. Both processes must not be mixed. In case a controller has a dedicated button "inclusion" this usually means that the use of this button turns the controller into the inclusion mode to include other devices. The mode to be included is therefore also referred to as **Learn Mode**. The manual of the controller shall provide information about both processes.

Figure 5.9 shows the process of including a controller as secondary controller. It is also possible to include a new controller into the network and hand over the primary controller function to this new controller. The process is the same but the primary controller needs to be turned into a special mode called **Primary Change**, **Primary Shift** or **Controller Shift**. The other controller will confirm the inclusion like any other normal slave. Please refer to the manual of the controller if and how this controller supports the "primary change" functions. Not all controllers have this function. Figure 5.10 shows the user interface of the software supporting this function.

Bring the prophet to the mountain or the mountain to the prophet?

Chapter 3.5.3 already explained the difference between the two main ways to organize networks: explorer frames and static update controller (SUC).
If

- the device to be included does not support explorer frame or
- the controller itself does not support explorer frame or

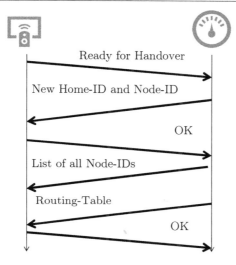

Figure 5.9: Controller-Replication

- there is no sufficient amount of explorer frame capable devices in the network to ensure routing of explorer frames,
the network will not benefit from the explorer frame and new
devices **must** be in direct radio range to the including controller.
There are two options for this:

1. Bringing all devices to the controller, include them and then
   install them in the final location.
2. Installing all devices at their final location and use a mobile
   controller for inclusion into the network.

Option (1) means to always change the network right after a
new device was included because this new device moves to a
different location within the network. This requires a network
rediscovery to be performed right after the device was installed at
its final location. The network rediscovery process will certainly
manage all mains powered devices and update all routing tables
accordingly but may fail for battery-operated devices for reasons

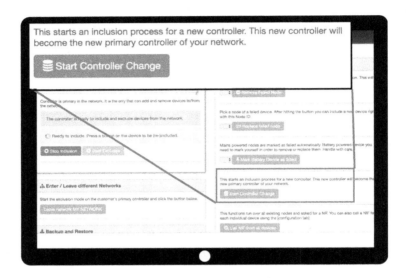

Figure 5.10: Example of Primary Change Function in PC software (Source: Expert User Interface of Z-Way by z-wave.me)

mentioned in Chapter 3.5.3. Additionally, all devices that will be mains operated and powered by fixed wires in the wall need to be powered temporarily just for inclusion when brought to the controller location.

Option (2) requires a mobile controller. Even then the management of battery-operated devices remains an issue.

What happens if I don't care at all about all this SUC and explorer frame stuff? Well, in 99% of the cases nothing will happen and the network will just work fine. However, according to Murphy's Law, it is the 1% that will kick in at the wrong moment and at the wrong place. So, it is recommended to understand what is going on behind the scenes to know what to do given a mixed set of devices and a network problem.

5.1.8   Inclusion of battery-operated devices

The big challenge of battery-operated devices is the deep sleep state. Once the battery is included the device should go right into deep sleep state but wake up when a button is pressed.

However, there are bad implementations of battery-operated devices that may cause trouble:

- They do not go into deep sleep right after batteries are inserted because they wait for an inclusion. If they get never included they will waste valuable battery lifetime.
- The device goes into deep sleep too fast.
- If nothing happens, they will go into deep sleep and not wake up anymore. It's impossible then to include the device.

The certification process meanwhile ensures that all new devices behave properly, but in order to avoid confusion, it's recommended to follow these guidelines:

1. Include every battery-operated device right after inserting the batteries. Make sure to configure a reasonable wake-up

time before the device goes into deep sleep state for the first time.

2. In case there is further configuration work needed, set a low wakeup interval first but make sure that you configure a longer battery-saving wakeup interval when all configuration work is finished. Alternatively, it is possible to wake up the device manually for finishing the configuration work.

3. Do not include and configure multiple devices at once and don't lose any time between inserting batteries and initial inclusion.

4. A reasonable wakeup time is a trade-off between two goals:
   - A very long wakeup interval will save battery capacity but may create problems in case of network rediscovery. The static controller may not receive anything from the battery device during the rediscovery and then assume the device as not functioning.
   - A very short wakeup time helps the controller to keep track of the device but costs battery lifetime.

5. The wakeup interval must be configured between the allowed boundaries. Refer to the manual of the manufacturer for more information about reasonable wakeup times. Typical wakeup intervals are between five minutes and a couple of days depending on the function of the device.

5.1.9   Interview Process

Right after inclusion the controller will perform the next step - called **Interview** as described in chapter 4.2.2. Interview describes a series of questions (from the controller) and answers (from the new device) to determine the functions of the new device. The interview must follow a defined pattern:

1. Determine if the new device supports security. If yes, establish a secure connection and ask the device for functions that may only be available within the security communication context. - e.g. door lock control.

2. Determine the version of all command classes reported within or outside the security communication context.

3. If the device reports a multichannel function, determine the number and characteristics of the different channels.

4. Run through all command classes and determine additional information such as sensor value and scale, association group number, size, and description.

Depending on the number of command classes this interview process can take quite long. The delay may become even worse if the new device is a FLiRS where it must be woken up using wakeup beams all the time again (see for information about FLiRS please refer to Chapter 3.3.2) and/or the communication uses the classic overhead-intense **Security Command Class V1** (for more information about Z-Wave security please refer to chapter 4.5).

The interview can not only be quit long it is also a very strict process. For most controllers one step is only started if the previous process step was finished successfully. The big amount of communication packets also makes the interview a stress test for both the device and the communication between this device and the controller. An incomplete interview may have one of the following reasons:

1. A combination of secure command class and/or FLiRS may make the interview too long so that the controller reaches a time out. Just restart the process.

2. Due to the heavy traffic and a weak link between the controller and the new device packets may get lost, resulting in stalling the interview process. Just restart it. If the interview always stops at the same point, there may be a different reason.

3. Battery operated devices may also go to sleep too early while the interview is not complete. Manually waking up the device usually helps.

4. In some cases, the new device may just not comply to the Z-Wave protocol 100 % resulting in failed communication.

If the interview process was completed successfully, this is a pretty good indicator that the device is doing fine and the communication link quality between device and controller is acceptable.

5.1.10   Configuration

The third step after inclusion and interview is the configuration of the device. For the reason and the general approach of configuration please refer to chapter 4.2.3. Graphical user interfaces provide a convenient way to set configuration values. The way a device is powered will determine when the changes become active:

- **Mains powered devices:** Right after saving or confirming the configuration parameter change in the user interface of the configuration tool.
- **FLIRS devices:** right after saving or confirming the configuration parameter change in the user interface of the configuration tool.
- **Battery-operated devices with periodical wake-up:** After the new configuration parameters are saved and the commands are queued up in the mailbox the device needs to wake up. This may take as long as the defined wakeup interval. Attention: If the wakeup interval was changed, the device is still in deep sleep for the time period of the previous setting. Only after successfully sending the new wakeup interval setting to the device the device will change its wakeup behavior. It is possible and recommended to manually wake up the device to speed up the process. Please refer to the manual of the device how to manually wake up the device.
- **Battery-powered portable controller:** After the new configuration parameters are saved and the commands are queued up in the mailbox the devices need to be manually woken up allowing the controller to store the new configuration values in the device.

Certain devices will not wake up if wakeup is not configured correctly. If they don't know where to send the wakeup notification, they will simply stay quiet. Other devices solve the situation by sending a wakeup notification as a broadcast command. As long as the primary controller is within wireless range of the device, broadcast will work fine.

5.1.11   Association and Scenes

It's possible to mix scenes and associations but it is recommended to stay with one system just for simplification.

Associations make much sense when there are simple and direct control relationships such as motion detector $\rightarrow$ light. It would only make the whole system more complicated to have this relation done using a gateway scene. Additionally, the direct control relationship between the motion detector and the light is more reliable—simply because there is less communication involved and the communication does not depend on the availability and function of the gateway.

As soon as there are more complex switching setups, the needed scenes in gateways are the better choice.

Similar to configuration settings, association settings need to be stored in the device before they become effective. For different behaviors on when this will happen after storing the association in the installer tool or in an IP gateway, please refer to Chapter 5.1.10.

5.2   Housekeeping - How to get a stable network?

Z-Wave is quite a robust wireless network that will work out of the box in the majority of the cases. Nevertheless, there are some housekeeping rules and guidelines to be considered. They are intended to make the network more stable and more robust.

5.2.1   Radio Layer

Here are some tips to avoid problems on the radio layer:

- Avoid metal wall boxes whenever possible. It is possible to run Z-Wave within a metal box but it may attenuate the radio signal. There are vendors that have designed products particularly for application in metal boxes but the majority of products may have problems in such an environment.
- Check the minimum wireless range and follow the recommendation given in section 2.3 in regard to radio shadow, installation height, reflection, etc. **Try to position all devices with a minimum distance of 30 cm from large metal constructions.**
- The fact that a Z-Wave network works properly during installation is no guarantee that it will work 24/7. There are plenty of ways to change the radio signal situation in a home. Even small changes like moving furniture or opening/closing a door may have impact. This is rare but not impossible.

Chapter 5.3 will provide an extensive description of the information and the process for trouble shooting using the Certified Installer Toolkit CIT provided by the Z-Wave Alliance.

5.2.2   Z-Wave Networking and Routing

There are few guidelines to optimize the routing function of the network.

- Avoid any traffic to nodes that will not respond anymore.
- Avoid any unneeded traffic to keep the air free for the real important messages.
- Make sure all devices always know how to communicate to each other.

This translates into the following practical recommendations:

1. Exclude devices that are no longer needed or that are moved outside the network. If one device is taken from the net-

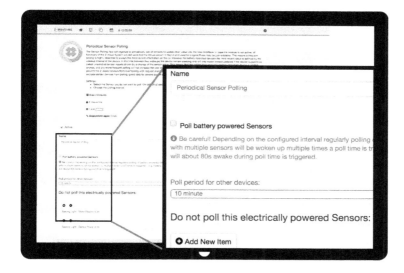

Figure 5.11: User Interface to allow individual polling (Source: Smarthome Interface of Z-Way by z-wave.me)

work, e.g. a wall plug by just unplugging, the device should be excluded from the network. Otherwise, this device is not reachable anymore and will create overhead traffic until it is marked as failed.

2. If a device is obviously failed or broken, remove it from the controller. Controllers typically have functions to remove failed nodes.

3. Don't forget to remove all disappeared nodes from all association groups where they were once included. The device having this association group will otherwise always try to communicate with these lost devices creating delay and waste valuable battery lifetime.

4. If a device is moved within the network, a network reorganization is always recommended.

5. Try to avoid longer routes since they increase the chance of routing failures. Z-Wave allows routes up to four hops (refer to Chapter 3.2 for details); however, longer routes with more than 2 intermediate nodes tend to be unstable.

6. The worst-case scenario for the routing algorithm is a device that is just in wireless range but drops out of direct range from time to time. Whenever the device is in direct wireless range, the direct range communication will be preferred and all the routes are discontinued. Whenever direct range does not work, the algorithms will need to redetect a valid route again, causing a lot of traffic in the network.

7. Reduce polling intensity. Every controller will poll all nodes from time to time to see if they are alive or to call certain status values. It is desired to poll very often to always have very updated values available in the controller. Heavy polling however creates a lot of traffic in the network and should therefore be limited. Some controllers only allow to set polling intervals for the whole network while others even allow to define polling behavior for every device. Figure 5.11 shows a user interface that allows to set polling

intervals.

(a) Choose a poll time that is reasonable. It's not recommended to poll more often than once per minute, even 5 minutes is a very reasonable number.

(b) Don't poll FLiRS devices.

(c) Try to enable unsolicited reporting of sensor values wherever possible. Most metering devices (power, temperature) allow to be configured so that they send sensor updates frequently or when changes occur. Make heavy use of these functions and limit the polling of the corresponding command classes.

(d) Sensors report the value of the actual moment while meters accumulate values. Meters should therefore not be polled more often than once per hour or even less.

(e) If there is already one device class polled delivering the status of a device e.g. switch binary command classes for a binary switch, there is no need to poll additional command classes - e.g. the basic command class - to get the very same value.

Network reorganization is also a good prevention task and it is recommended after any change of the network (include device, exclude devices, remove failed nodes, move nodes). Please be aware that changes in the environment such as new furniture may also change the wireless communication environment. A regular network reorganization is therefore a good practice to keep the network healthy and stable. The net-net of these recommendations are:

- **Avoid metal surfaces closer than 30 cm.**
- **Use explorer frame capable device as much as you can.**
- **Avoid wireless links that are at the edge of direct wireless range.**
- **Get rid of all devices not used anymore.**

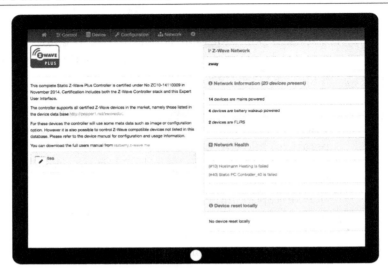

Figure 5.12: Expert User Interface of Z-Way

- **Perform a network reorganization after every change of the network.**

5.3 Trouble Shooting with CIT Tool or Z-Way Expert UI

Troubleshooting a Z-Wave network works along the lines of the communication stack as mentioned in Chapter 1.3. Problems can happen on the radio layer, the networking layer, and the application layer. To identify and fix problems, it makes sense to work bottom up through the network stack issues. Unfortunately, only very few controllers provide all the necessary information to troubleshoot these different layers. Among the controllers offering these functions built-in are

- Z-Way by z-wave.me,

Figure 5.13: CIT device (Source: Z-Wave Alliance)

- Popp Hub,
- Dome Z-Box,
- ...

They use a middleware called Z-Way that offers the so-called Z-Wave Experts User Interface as shown in Figure 5.12. Usually, you access this user interface by pointing a web browser to

$$http://IP.OF.CONTROLLER : 8083/expert$$

All options and dialogs mentioned below are available on this interface.

For all other gateways the Z-Wave Alliance offers a tool that can be used as companion to a gateway already installed. The 'Certified Installer Toolkit CIT' is available for all Z-Wave Alliance Members [Alliance2017] that are installers and have passed the Z-Wave Alliance Installer Training. The CIT is a fully functional controller itself but it is used to act as a kind of consultant to the network in trouble. It gets included as secondary controller but will then stay silent only analyzing the network situation and eavesdropping on the packet flow. Once the job is done, the CIT can be excluded from the network and can be reused in other networks.

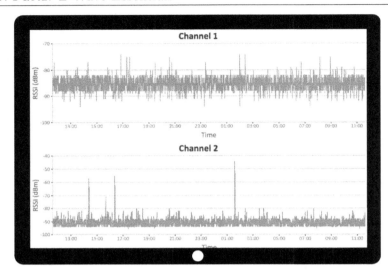

Figure 5.14: Background Noise (Source: Certified Installer Toolkit)

Users of gateways with Z-Way Expert User Interface do not need this tool because they have all the functions right on the gateway all the time.

5.3.1 Radio Layer

Problems on the radio layer come from interference and noise generated by defect or nonconforming electrical gear causing electromagnetic emissions (baby monitor, old cordless phones, wireless speakers, motors, etc.). Other Z-Wave networks with unusual high traffic can also be a root cause of problems. It is also possible that certain other wireless networking services (first and foremost cellular network G4 routers or base stations, also called LTE) may cause interference if they are too closed to the Z-Wave network [Paetz2013].

The menu item **'Background Noise'** offers a view chart dis-

Figure 5.15: Realtime Measurement of Background-Noise (Source: Certified Installer Toolkit)

playing the background noise on the two communication channels used by Z-Wave. Channel 1 refers to the 9.6 Kbit/s and 40 kbit/s communication modes, channel 2 points to the 100kbit/s data rate. Figure 5.14 shows this viewgraph. There is an obvious floor of noise with some other "needles." This noise floor—in Figure 5.14 at about -85 dBm for channel 1 and -90 dBm for channel 2—is the minimum level a Z-Wave transceivers signal must surpass in order to be decoded by the Z-Wave receiver.

The lower the noise level the better the wireless situation. Noise levels below - 95 dBm are very good, levels above -70 dBm are very bad.

Please note that this noise level is measured right on the controllers location or wherever the CIT is positioned. It may make sense to move the measuring device around to see the noise level at different locations. Since the **"Background Noise"** viewgraph is only updated once per minute, you may want to use the tool **"Noise Gauge"**, as shown in Figure 5.15. In this case, the display is updated every two seconds.

Figure 5.16: Powerbank to power the CIT for mobile use

If the noise floor is too high, you need to find the source of the noise. The CIT can be used as mobile device too, thanks to the built-in Wi-Fi. In this case, it needs to be powered with a power bank as shown in Figure 5.16.

Walking around with the Noise Gauge enabled may help to track down the jamming device. The closer the CIT gets to the source of the noise, the higher the background noise level will be.

The "needles" above the noise floor show communication from other Z-Wave networks around. Having this is not a real problem unless other networks generate heavy traffic. A rule of thumb is that there should not be more than 30 % of the time allocated by traffic of other Z-Wave networks. If there is more traffic, there will be a need to troubleshoot the other Z-Wave network first. The chart **Network Statistics**, as shown in Figure 5.17, shows a ratio of own traffic versus traffic seen from other networks.

5.3.2   Network Layer - Devices

Devices can have two faulty states:

- They are dead, removed, faulty, stolen, etc. In case of a mains operated device the central controller or CIT will

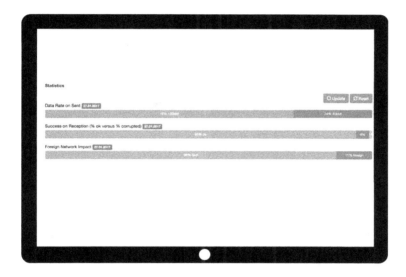

Figure 5.17: Network Statistics Display (Source: Certified Installer Toolkit)

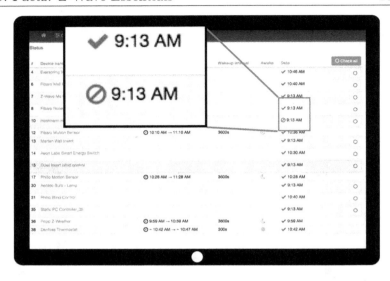

Figure 5.18: Status Page Expert User Interface / CIT (Source: Certified Installer Toolkit)

sooner or later find out that the device is not responding. It will put the device in the failed node list (for more information about the failed node list please refer to chapter 3.4.2). The **Device Status Overview** as shown in Figure 5.18 indicates if a device is failed or not. It is possible to make a test if the device is working.

• The device is working but constantly sending unsolicited messages. This is a rare but not impossible behavior. The simplest way to find out is to look into the packet sniffer. Figure 5.19 shows the **Sniffer View** of the Z-Wave Expert UI or CIT.

Another option to detect faulty devices is the **Timing Info View** only available in Z-Wave Expert UI:

Figure 5.20 shows this view. The timing information lists one entry for every communication between the controller and the

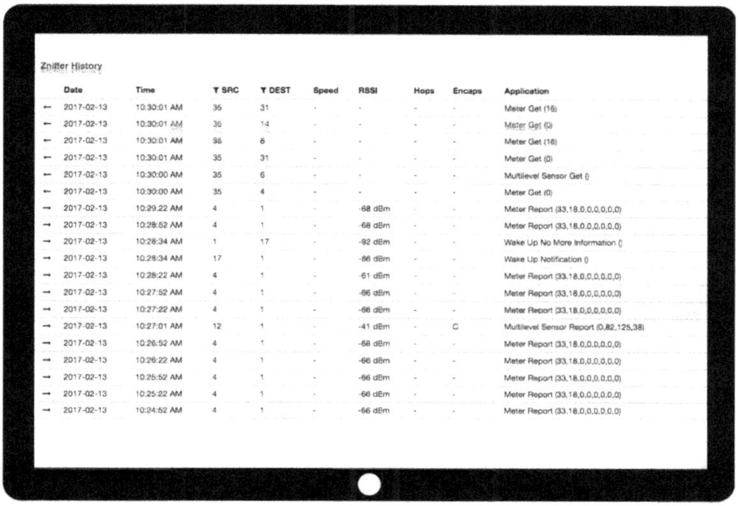

Zniffer History

	Date	Time	SRC	DEST	Speed	RSSI	Hops	Encaps	Application
←	2017-02-13	10:30:01 AM	35	31	-	-	-	-	Meter Get (16)
←	2017-02-13	10:30:01 AM	35	14	-	-	-	-	Meter Get (0)
←	2017-02-13	10:30:01 AM	35	6	-	-	-	-	Meter Get (16)
←	2017-02-13	10:30:01 AM	35	31	-	-	-	-	Meter Get (0)
←	2017-02-13	10:30:00 AM	35	6	-	-	-	-	Multilevel Sensor Get ()
←	2017-02-13	10:30:00 AM	35	4	-	-	-	-	Meter Get (0)
→	2017-02-13	10:29:22 AM	4	1	-	-68 dBm	-	-	Meter Report (33,18,0,0,0,0,0,0)
→	2017-02-13	10:28:52 AM	4	1	-	-68 dBm	-	-	Meter Report (33,18,0,0,0,0,0,0)
→	2017-02-13	10:28:34 AM	1	17	-	-92 dBm	-	-	Wake Up No More Information ()
→	2017-02-13	10:28:34 AM	17	1	-	-86 dBm	-	-	Wake Up Notification ()
→	2017-02-13	10:28:22 AM	4	1	-	-61 dBm	-	-	Meter Report (33,18,0,0,0,0,0,0)
→	2017-02-13	10:27:52 AM	4	1	-	-66 dBm	-	-	Meter Report (33,18,0,0,0,0,0,0)
→	2017-02-13	10:27:22 AM	4	1	-	-66 dBm	-	-	Meter Report (33,18,0,0,0,0,0,0)
→	2017-02-13	10:27:01 AM	12	1	-	-41 dBm	-	C	Multilevel Sensor Report (0,82,125,38)
→	2017-02-13	10:26:52 AM	4	1	-	-68 dBm	-	-	Meter Report (33,18,0,0,0,0,0,0)
→	2017-02-13	10:26:22 AM	4	1	-	-66 dBm	-	-	Meter Report (33,18,0,0,0,0,0,0)
→	2017-02-13	10:25:52 AM	4	1	-	-66 dBm	-	-	Meter Report (33,18,0,0,0,0,0,0)
→	2017-02-13	10:25:22 AM	4	1	-	-66 dBm	-	-	Meter Report (33,18,0,0,0,0,0,0)
→	2017-02-13	10:24:52 AM	4	1	-	-66 dBm	-	-	Meter Report (33,18,0,0,0,0,0,0)

Figure 5.19: Packet Sniffer (Source: Certified Installer Toolkit)

device. The number refers to the time (in x * 10 ms) the message took before being confirmed, the color gives a rough indication of what happened:

- Green: Successful communication with device in direct wireless range.
- Black: Successful communication with device using a route.
- Red: Failed communication (after a total of nine attempts).

Figure 5.20 shows the situation in a network just installed. It can be seen that there is only communication with few devices, e.g. no polling of sensors, etc. While this is not a problem, the chart shows that devices 4, 6, and 31 are in direct range and all communication works perfectly well (green, low number). Device 14 seems to be a real problem child. The controller tries all the time to reach this node but always fails. At some point in time, the controller will accept that node 31 is dead and put him into the "failed node list."

Figure 5.20: Paket timing of a fresh Z-Wave network (Source: Expert User Interface of Z-Way by z-wave.me)

Figure 5.21: Paket timing of an aged Z-Wave network (Source: Expert User Interface of Z-Way by z-wave.me)

Figure 5.21 shows a network that is a bit more complex, has more communication and is aged. Again node 20 is a defect device that just needs to be replaced. The following interesting patterns can be seen:

- Node 5 can be reached via routes only but one time not even this worked. There was some error. It is possible that the failure of node 20 caused his and then the system found an alternative route.

- Node 6 seems to be in direct range with very stable communication but from time to time there is a failed communication. Since this is a battery-operated node, it is highly likely that the last communication with the device reaches this device while already in deep sleep state. This does not harm the communication at all but is worth monitoring.

- Node 15 switches between direct communication and routed communication. It seems to be right on the edge of having a stable direct link but sometimes - may be when doors are open/closed - the direct range does not work anymore.
  Anyway, the controller seems to understand that direct range is the by far best option and constantly tries to reach the node in direct range. The same pattern can be seen for nodes 29 and 31.

- Node 24 has an interesting history. For some time, there was a stable direct range communication but then it got worse and worse to a point where communication even failed. However, the link recovered and the very last communication was again direct, but with a slight delay of 80 ms.

5.3.3   Network Layer - Weak or Wrong Routes

It is the best already knowing the troublemaking devices. In this case the status of device can be checked quickly and it is possible to dig deeper into the routing layer. Figure 5.22 shows the routing table of a controller. Technically this is not a rout-

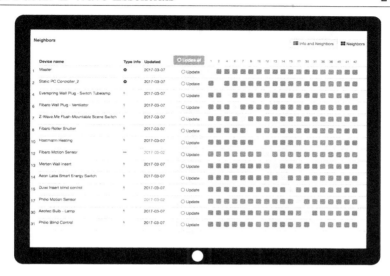

Figure 5.22: Neighbor-Table of a controller (Source: Certified Installer Toolkit)

ing table but a matrix indicating the wireless neighborhoods of devices. Nevertheless, this a good starting point to investigate deeper. Having many neighbors is a good thing since the routing algorithm has many options in case something goes wrong. On the other hand, just having one other route to communicate to the rest of the network may cause trouble if this route is faulty or moved.

The next step is to check individual routes. The configuration page of every device offers a link health check that allows testing the links from this very device to its neighbors.

While the neighborhood table shows if two devices are neighbors the link test checks how good this wireless links is in reality. Unfortunately, not all but an increasing number of devices on the market support this link test. Figure 5.23 shows this dialog within the Z-Wave Expert UI or CIT. Every link has a color

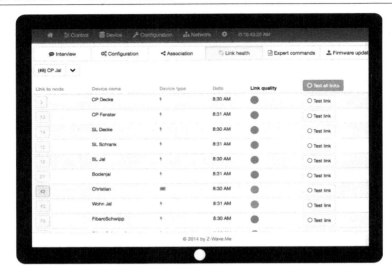

Figure 5.23: Link test of a node (Source: Certified Installer Toolkit)

indicator (green = ok, red = bad, grey = unknown) and a time stamp that shows when this test was done the last time.

Please note that the link check is a momentary analysis only and does not give any information about the history of the link quality.

This can only be taken from the timing info chart above or from the so-called **Poltorak-Chart**[1].

The **Poltorak-Chart** is an extremely powerful, informative but the same time very complex viewgraph of the network situation in a home. The chart visualizes the possible links between the nodes and how they are used. If provided by the devices the chart will furthermore show complete routes and the signal strength of the individual links of a route. However only devices with SDK greater or equal to 6.71 will provide this additional information.

---

[1]Named after its inventor Serguei Poltorak - Kudos!

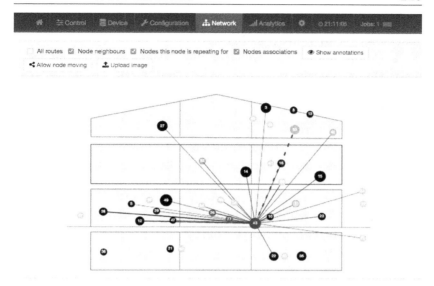

Figure 5.24: Poltorak-Chart (Source: Expert User Interface of Z-Way by z-wave.me)

For more information about SDKs please refer to 6.2.

Initially all nodes are displayed with equal distances. It is possible to drag and drop the nodes to match the distances between them with the real distances. This will always work quite well if the Z-Wave network is in one floor only. A 2D map can be uploaded as background image to support the mapping. If the network is distributed on multiple floors it is recommended to do a best guess to keep the round initial view.

Figure 5.24 shows a typical chart. By clicking on a certain node and then moving the mouse over it again, it is possible to analyse the traffic from and to this very node. This allows focusing on the situation of this node only.

The lines between the nodes represent the wireless connections and the communication between the nodes. The following information is encoded in these lines:

- Color: The color indicates the wireless signal strength of the connection if it can be measured. Red means a very high wireless signal. The device is likely very closed or in direct sight of the each other. A black color means a standard wireless strength, gray indicates that the received signal strength (RSSI value) is not known.
- Thickness: The Thickness of the line indicates the amount of traffic running over this line. This can be direct communication between the two links or routed traffic. If a route exist there will be a single pixel line. Every line thicker than a pixel shows real traffic.
- Dotted versus solid: A dotted line indicates that this link is sometimes just not working.

The **Poltorak-Chart** is almost a scientific tool rather than a debug tool, since it gives a very deep insight into the routing and communication situation of a network. However, the options to fix detected problems are limited. It is possible to remove obstacles, reorganize the network (see chapter 3.4.3 for information about network reorganization) or add mode mains operated devices to stabilize the network.

5.3.4   Application Layer Settings

In the application layer, there is usually no malfunction of a device but wrong configurations. The Z-Wave Expert UI and partly the CIT allow double checking certain settings to ensure proper functions.

Polling

Heavy polling of devices causes network traffic leading to delays. A simple look on the sniffer as shown in Figure 5.19 reveal if there is too much polling. Chapter 5.2.2 gives guidelines about

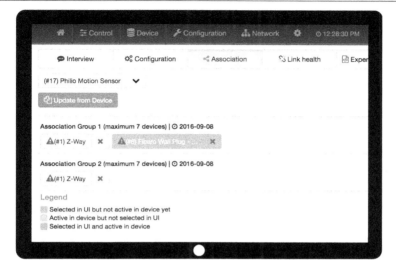

Figure 5.25: Association Dialog (Source: Expert User Interface of Z-Way by z-wave.me)

polling.

Dead Associations

Association enable direct communication between devices. In case there are more than one device in an association group they will receive a command one after each other. A very common problem is that associations are set during the built-up of the network and later certain devices are removed or simply fail. As long as this disappeared node is still in an association group, the device will always try to communicate to this node first before communicating to other nodes. The result is a delay. The device-specific configuration overview as shown in Figure 5.25 displays all association that are set. It is possible to recall the current associations from the device and to remove or set associations.

Wrong Wakeup Settings

Wrong wakeup settings may either result in too much traffic draining the battery, or in too slow response to sensor update requests or configuration changes. The status overview page as shown in Figure 5.18 gives a simple overview of the wakeup settings of the different battery-operated sleeping devices. The device-specific configuration settings allow changing these settings. Besides the wakeup interval, the setting also allows setting/changing the Node-ID of the controller holding the mailbox of this device. This setting must reflect the correct situation in the network.

5.3.5 Summary

Table 5.1 summarizes the possible *'ten root causes of Z-Wave network problems'* and suggestions how to fix them.

Table 5.2 shows a comparison between the functions available on the CIT versus functions available on Z-Way Expert-UI.

5.4 Known Problems

In general, Z-Wave is a mature and easy-to-use technology. However, it needs to be considered that users have to deal with technologies of different manufacturers, different quality of documentation, and different quality of products.

> Z-Wave guarantees
> interoperability
> but not quality.

With over 1700 different products (as of 2017) introduced over the course of 15 years, there are certain differences in functionality of devices. Here is a list of typical challenges, pitfalls and problems:

No.	Cause	How to find ?	How to fix ?
1	Noise by other transmitters	Background Noise Chart	Find them and turn them off
2	Noise by other Z-Wave networks	Background Noise Chart, Network Statistics	Talk to the neighbor ;-)
3	Faulty devices	Status Page, Failed Node	Remove them or replace them.
4	Crazy Devices (always sending)	Sniffer	Remove them or replace them
5	Weak Link	Neighbor-Table, Link Health in Configuration Page	Add more routing nodes, move devices
6	Heavy Fading	Timing Infos	Network Reorganization, more devices
7	Wrong Routing	Timing Infos	Network Reorganization
8	Wrong Polling	Sniffer	Change and Save
9	Wrong Wakeup Intervals	Status Page	Change and Save
10	Dead Nodes in Assoc. Groups	Association display in Configuration Page	Change and Save

Table 5.1: Troubleshooting on Z-Wave networks

Function	CIT	Expert UI
Background Noise	yes	yes
Noise-Gauge	yes	no
Network Statistics	yes	yes
Network Status	mains powered devices only	yes
Sniffer	shows pakets seen	shows own pakets only
Timing Info	no	yes
Neighbor-Table	no	yes
Link-Quality	mains powered devices only	yes
Wakeup-Behavior	no	yes
Battery Status	no	yes
Associations	mains powered devices only	yes

Table 5.2: Comparison betwen CIT and Expert UI

5.4.1   Mismatch of Language

The Z-Wave alliance enforces the use for common language for
the most critical processes and functions of Z-Wave:

- Inclusion and Exclusion
- Association
- Configuration
- Meshing and Routing

Every term beyond this short list may be interpreted differently
by different manufacturers. Manuals in languages other than
English bear another reason for confusion, since local-language
translations even of the core terms of Z-Wave are not monitored
and controlled by the Z-Wave Alliance.

5.4.2   Mismatch of functions

In order to simplify the use of Z-Wave, some manufacturers have
combined the steps of inclusion and association into one step.
Particularly, remote controls may just allow *including a new device to a group*. This is a description of an association. Knowl-
edgeable Z-Wave users will miss the first step always needed—the
inclusion. The remote control combines both functions into one.
This is not necessarily a bad idea, but it may create confusion.

5.4.3   No forward compatibility

The core value of Z-Wave is interoperability. This is maintained
among others by ensure that all new devices are 100 percent
backward-compatible to existing products. As a result, it is still
possible to use a first-generation product that is 10 years old in
todays networks. Considering the product lifecycles in information technology, this is a remarkable achievement. Figure 5.26
shows one of the first Z-Wave products of the first generation,
developed in the early 2000s. It is no longer in production, but
the device will work well even in modern networks and can be

Figure 5.26: 1st generation Z-Wave product, made by Advanced Control Technologies

controlled by any Z-Wave controller that has ever been designed. However, compatibility is only a one-way street. It is impossible to develop products that will be **compatible to functions** that **will be invented in the future**. This does not violate interoperability and compatibility but may be perceived as such.

Example:

A remote control developed in 2007 can operate switches, dimmers, and control motors to move blinds or doors. It was certified and works well. Around 2009/2010, a new category of lighting devices became available—multicolor LEDs. Multicolor LEDs can adapt the temperature of the light to the user needs or can be turned into almost any color imaginable.

The Z-Wave alliance has reacted to this new product category and has specified a way how Z-Wave controller can define the color of a multicolor LED. This command class `Color Control Command Class` was finalized in 2010 and right after finalizing, the first products using this technology hit the streets.

The multicolor-LEDs are backward-compatible. They can still be switched and dimmed the way a light was switched or dimmed before. A user can use his old remote control to dim and switch the LED, but he cannot choose the LEDs' light color by this remote control because this color picking function did not exist when the remote control was developed. Users may perceive this as incompatibility.

5.4.4   Multi Channels versus Multi Instances

There is no rule without exception and while Z-Wave maintains backward compatibility at almost any cost, the exception is called `Multi Instance Command Class`. Here is the story:
Initially, it was assumed that every device only has one function of its kind. A switch device has one relay, a dimmer device has one dimmer. Later, it became obvious that it makes sense to have similar functions in one device. A good example would be a power strip where all the outlets will be switches. The power strip will be controlled by one single Z-Wave transceiver, but the `Switch Binary` command class does not support multiple switching functions.

To maintain backward compatibility of all devices supporting and controlling binary switches, another command class was introduced that allows differentiating multiple instances of a device. This device class was called `Multi Instance Command Class`.

After the introduction of this command class, it turned out that the command created more problems than it solved and quickly a second version of the command class was developed. To differentiate from the first version, it was called `Multi Channel Command Class`. For some intermediate time, devices with the `Multi Instance Command Class` were still accepted in certification, but meanwhile the command class is really abandoned and must not be used anymore. Fortunately, only a couple of devices were ever introduced using the old `Multi Instance Command Class`, among them were a lot of devices from the German manufacturer Merten, now part of Schneider Electric.

Consequently, there are quite a few incompatibilities between `Multi Instance Command Class` products and all other Z-Wave products. Very few gateways, such as Z-Way from z-wave.me[Zme2017], support both `Multi Instance Command Class` and `Multi Channel Command Class`, but the majority just ignores the old `Multi Instance Command Class`.

Along with the introduction of the `Multi Channel Command Class`, a new command class for handling associations with these devices was needed. The `Multi Channel Association Command Class` extends the normal association command class allowing setting different instances of a device into an association group.

5.4.5 Sins from the past

When Z-Wave was introduced to the market in the early 2000s, the certification was less strict so that devices were certified that would not get a certification granted anymore. These old devices may create problems because they simply don't follow the standard in all aspects. Fortunately, these products more and more disappear. However, some of them may still be around.

5.4.6 IP-Gateways

Smart homes are at the intersection of two different worlds. On the one hand, there is the conservative world of facility management, house installation, and installers. They do not have the intention to "play" with products for too long. Their technology is stable and well proven.

On the other hand, there is the information technology, namely the software business. Here we see frequent product updates, software patches, and release changes.

IP gateways certainly belong to the group of IT equipment. Frequent software updates, feature enhancements, bug fixes, etc. cause a constant change in the system if the user wants to follow all the updates. It is not uncommon that a firmware for an IP gateway gets released just followed by another one after few days fixing a bug that was just introduced in the first place.

5.4.7   Weak Check Sum

Chapter 3.1.5 describes the Checksum algorithm used in Z-Wave and discusses the weakness of the legacy solution. Particularly for data collection and large messages the weak checksum results in wrong transmissions from time to time. Z-Wave has therefore introduced a new system that protects metering and sensor data with another 16-bit strong checksum. In order to use this new strong protection of data, both the device and the controller need to support it. Since most Z-Wave devices now support communication Channel 3 with its strong CRC 16 checksum, this problem is almost history as well.

5.4.8   Turnkey-Solutions

It is the very natural interest of suppliers to sell as many devices to customers as possible. Hence, they try to lock-in customers to their solutions so that they can generate follow-up revenue once the customer bought the initial solution. This is in conflict with the Z-Wave principle that devices should work together regardless of brand or origin.

The certification process ensures that the basic interoperability is maintained, but vendors always find new ways to differentiate their devices from other vendors' so that people prefer their own brand. A very common way is to offer a selection of their own devices for inclusion only. Z-Wave certification requires that all devices be included, but vendors are creative in hiding this generic inclusion option. Sometimes only a call to the manufacturer's support hotline gives the needed information to benefit from the interoperability promise of Z-Wave.

Chapter 6

Special topics around Z-Wave

6.1 Legal situation

The Z-Wave communication architecture comprises various parts with different legal statuses.

Figure 6.1 gives an overview of these different parts of Z-Wave.

- PHY: The physical layer that deals with frequencies, framing, error detection etc. is specified by the ITU-T under G.9959 and therefore public domain.

- MAC: The media access layer that deals with Node IDs, Home IDs, addresses, retransmission etc. is specified by the ITU-T under G.9959 and therefore public domain.

- NET: The network layer that deals with Inclusion, Routing and Network reorganization remains intellectual property of Silicon Labs and is offered royalty-free to all manufacturers that want to develop and manufacture Z-Wave devices.

- APP: The application layer that defines what a product is doing and how it acts is owned by the manufacturer of the device. However, the implementation of this layer must use

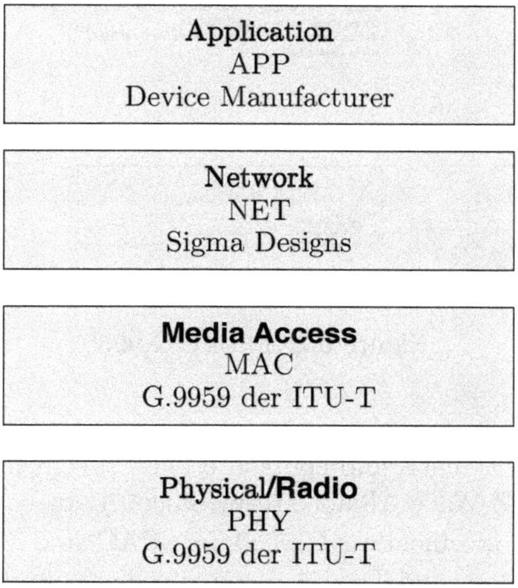

Figure 6.1: Different layers of Z-Wave and its legal status

INTERNATIONAL TELECOMMUNICATION UNION

ITU-T   **G.9959**
TELECOMMUNICATION   (02/2012)
STANDARDIZATION SECTOR
OF ITU

SERIES G: TRANSMISSION SYSTEMS AND MEDIA,
DIGITAL SYSTEMS AND NETWORKS
Access networks – In premises networks

**Short range narrowband digital
radiocommunication transceivers – PHY & MAC
layer specifications**

CAUTION !
PREPUBLISHED RECOMMENDATION
This prepublication is an unedited version of a recently approved Recommendation.
It will be replaced by the published version after editing. Therefore, there will be
differences between this prepublication and the published version.

Figure 6.2: ITU-T G.9959

the device class and command class specification provided
by the Z-Wave Alliance resp. Silicon Labs.
The ITU-T Specification G.9959 for MAC and PHY and the
Command Class and Device Type specifications for the application layer are freely available and all implementations of the
protocol are free of patent claims or any other royalty payment
needs. Figure 6.2 shows the cover page of the official ITU-T spec.

6.1.1   Important Patents of Z-Wave

The networking layer of Z-Wave is protected among others by
the following patents, all held by Silicon Labs:

- US6856236: *RF home automation system comprising nodes
  with dual functionality, filed April 25th, 2001* A system

that has multiple devices with receiver, transmitter, a CPU and memory to store identifiers; a controller with receiver, transmitter, memory to store the identifiers of the devices and another memory to hold the controllers own identifier information, and a processor one or more devices that can act as repeaters by receiving information, processing them and sending them out again and one or more devices that act as I/O devices, means generating an event signal in response to received input.

- US6879806: *System and a method of building routing tables and for routing signals in an automation system, filed June 1st, 2001* A system defined in US6856236 that is able to build neighborhood tables that can be used for routing.
- US6980080: *RF home automation system with replicable controllers, filed April 25, 2001* A system defined in US6856236 that allows transferring routing information from one controller to another controller.
- US7680041: *Node Repair in a mesh network, files Mar, 9th, 2007* The use of SUC and SIS in a meshed network.

6.1.2   Important Patents challenging Z-Wave

The Z-Wave core definitions are not subject to any patent dispute. However, real implementations of Z-Wave networks use certain architectures or processes that are covered by third-party patents. This has led to several patent litigations and licensing agreements of Z-Wave manufacturers.

The Lutron Patent

The US company Lutron has filed the patent 5.905.442 in the mid-1990s describing the wireless control of lights from wall switches. The patent relates specifically to wireless networks with mesh routing functions. Hence, a lot of the simpler wireless technologies on the market do not infringe on the patent but Z-Wave does.

The key patent claim No. 1 describes: *1. Apparatus for controlling at least one electrical device by remote control comprising: at least one control device coupled to the electrical device by a wire connection for providing power to the electrical device, the control device having a controllably conductive device for adjusting the status of said electrical device, the control device further having a manual actuator for adjusting the status of the electrical device, the control device further having a radio frequency transmitter/receiver and antenna coupled thereto for adjusting the status of the electrical device in response to control information in a radio frequency signal, the transmitter/receiver being coupled to the antenna of the control device for receiving the radio frequency signal and for transmitting a status radio frequency signal having status information therein regarding the status of the electrical device as affected by the control information and the manual actuator; a master control unit having at least one actuator and status indicator thereon, the master unit comprising a transmitter/receiver for transmitting a radio frequency signal having the control information therein to control the status of said at least one electrical device and for receiving the status information from the control device, the status indicator indicating the status of the electrical device in response to the status information; and a repeater transmitter/receiver for receiving the radio frequency signal from the master unit and transmitting the control information to the control device and for receiving the status information from the control device and transmitting the status information to the master unit.*

Every sending of a status signal as result of a local status change of a wireless device in a routed network infringes this patent. This is the reason why manufacturers of Z-Wave devices intentionally did not implement a status report function as a result of local status change.

Consequently, the gateway does not recognize a local status change of the device and will continue to show a wrong status of this particular device.

Meanwhile, people found—as almost always—a way to solve the problem without infringing on the Lutron patent. Devices such as wall switches, wall dimmers, outlet plug switches, and dimmers with a local button offer an association group to operate remote devices simultaneously to the local operation. Using the local button is not only switching the local state but is causing to send a switching command to an association group. The main difference from the patent-protected scenario is that there is no longer a status report (protected by patent) but a switching command (allowed by the patent). Besides other switches that can be switched simultaneously with the button on one switch, the gateway itself may also be a target device. In this case, the gateway must emulate the behavior of a standard switch to be able to receive switching commands. Receiving a switching command from a wall switch will not cause the gateway to switch on a lamp but to immediately check the status of this particular switch and, subsequently, update the switch state on the gateways GUI. One other method is to just send a `Hail` command that may be used to pull the device status.

The Sipco Patents

Sipco is a very small US company that has filed certain inventions around the use of mesh networking back in the year of 2000. Although these systems were likely never manufactured or sold the description and patents around these ideas provide very valuable intellectual property to the inventor. The main patents hold by SIPCO and used against Z-Wave device manufacturers are:

- US6891838: System and Method for monitoring and controlling residential devices
- US6914893: System and Method for monitoring and controlling remote devices
- US7103511: Wireless Communication Networks for providing remote monitoring of devices

The claims of these patents are focused on the access of a meshed short range wireless network via a gateway to the internet. This means that all manufacturers of IP gateways or their customers are subject to a possible violation of this patent.

All patents mentioned in the sections above are valid in the USA only. There are no such patent problems known in Europe.

6.2 SDKs

All Z-Wave devices run a firmware that consists of two parts: There is a fixed part delivered by Sigma Designs that covers all network related functions and there is a vendor specific part, that the vendors define and implement according to the Z-Wave specification. The part provided by Silicon Labs is called **Systems Development Kit (SDK)** and has different release numbers. Certain versions of this SDK introduced new functions. These SDKs are always backward compatible but the new functions are then available only for this SDK and subsequent SDK numbers. The following important release versions of SDKs exist:

- SDK 3.0x: First Generation of Z-Wave ASIC ZW0102
- SDK 3.20: Introduces Static Update Controller (SUC) in 2003
- SDK 3.40: SUC ID Server (SIS) in 2005
- SDK 4.00: Second Generation of Z-Wave ASIC ZW0201 in 2005
- SDK 4.20: Silent Acknowledge in 2006
- SDK 5.0x: Third Generation of Z-Wave ASIC ZW0301 in 2007
- SDK 4.5x: Explorer frame plus network wide inclusion in 2009
- SDK 6.0x: Fourth Generation of Z-Wave ASIC ZW0401 in 2010
- SDK 6.5x: Fifth Generation of Z-Wave ASIC 2013
- SDK 6.7x: New Security Architecture S2

Figure 6.3: SDK Version shown in Z-Way Software (Source: Certified Installer Toolkit)

- SDK 6.8x: Introduction of Smart Start

All SDKs before 3.40 can be considered as obsolete and only very few products are still in the market based on these SDKs. All SDKs from 4.20 but not 4.5x and the SDK 5.x and 6.x share the same support for the basic Z-Wave network functions and processes, namely the SUC/SIS support. The SDKs 4.5x plus all SDKs from 6.x add explorer frame support that greatly enhance the way the network is self-reorganizing in case of changes. All products based on these SDKs are 100 % backward compatible to the older SDKs.

Figure 6.3 shows how a Z-Wave software indicates the SDK version used for the Z-Wave transceiver IC.

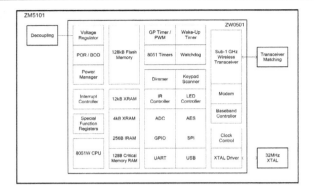

Figure 6.4: Z-Wave ASIC Building blocks (Source: Silicon Labs)

6.3   How to develop Z-Wave devices

6.3.1   Hardware

All Z-Wave devices are based on a Z-Wave ASIC from Silicon Labs. The company offer various versions of the Z-Wave IC but they all contain the very same core elements.

Figure 6.4 shows the internal building blocks of the Z-Wave-ASIC. The key components are the 8051-compatible 8-bit microcontroller with memory and the radio frontend. There are also quite a few peripheral interfaces allowing to build a lot of different application using just the ASIC as such. The versions of the ASIC differ by the number and type of I/O signals available on the packaging and other peripheral components already integrated into the packaging too.

Figure 6.5 shows the complete schematic of a very typical Z-Wave application using one single button or switch. The product could be a door/window sensor where the switch is a magnet operated hall switch element. It is also possible that this application is a panic button with one switch or a simple single-button remote

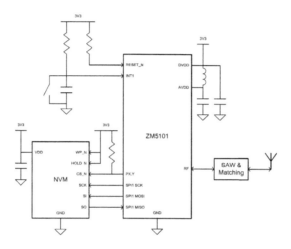

Figure 6.5: Schematics of a single button controller using the Z-Wave ASIC (Source: Silicon Labs)

control. The schematic is remarkably simple. The reset and the switch I/O have a pull-up resistor, the capacity parallel to the switch will suppress glitches. The antenna matching usually consists of two capacitors and the SAW antenna filter (For more information about the use of SAW antenna filter, please refer to Chapter 2.2.3.). Some capacities on the power supply complete the design. The schematic in Figure 6.5 has one additional external component: an EEPROM to store additional values. This component is required to support firmware update *"Over the Air (OTA)"*. If this function is not desired, the EEPROM (NVM = Non volatile memory) can be removed, leaving just 11 components in total to implement a useful Z-Wave product.

Other products may connect analog or digital sensor to the IC, control relays or MOSFETs/TRIACs (for dimmers) by I/O, or even have a second microcontroller for other purposes.

However, thanks to the functions already available within the ASIC, most current Z-Wave products do not have much complicated hardware but use the ASIC alone.

6.3.2   Firmware

The microcontroller contains a firmware. This firmware consists of two parts:

- The fixed library with all the network control and management.
- The device and vendor specific part with the implementation of the command classes and the application logic.

To develop the firmware a System Development Kit (SDK) is needed. For more information about Z-Wave SDKs please refer also to Chapter 6.2.

This can be purchased by Silicon Labs or certain distributors such as digikey.com. The SDK as shown in Figure 6.6 contains a lot of useful tools and information:

- The precompiled libraries for various types of devices.

Figure 6.6: Z-Wave System Development Kit Hardware (Source: Silicon Labs)

- The C programming environment with examples, header files, tools, helper codes, etc.
- Extensive documentation about the hardware, software, use cases, etc.
- Some sample hardware that can be used as controller, test device etc.
- A wireless sniffer capable to reading all wireless signals in the air.
- A flashing tool to program the firmware to the chip.
- Access to an online site with more information such as documentation, sample code, application notes, errata, etc.
- Standard software applications like a PC controller, the flashing tool, the sniffer application and some other tools.

Parts of the SDK are skeleton codes that simplify the firmware development. They are essentially ready-to-use code parts, allowing extension with their own code in three different locations:

Figure 6.7: ZUNO (Source: Z-Wave.Me)

- `ApplicationProgrammHandler`: to place code that is executed every time when the CPU is running.
- `ApplicationMessageHandler`: to place code to react on incoming Z-Wave messages (like sending an `REPORT` when a `GET` command is received).
- `Interrupthandler`: to place code to handle external interrupts such a buttons pressed etc.

While this description suggests that firmware development is an easy task—it is not! Even experienced developers need several months to get started with a new Z-Wave product and the complexity of the Z-Wave protocol and the very long list of requirements to pass certification require extensive knowledge and experience to write Z-Wave firmware.

6.3.3 ZUNO

One elegant way to develop own Z-Wave devices is called ZUNO. ZUNO (zuno.z-wave.me) is a small test board as shown in Figure 6.7 that brings out all I/O signals to pin headers that can be

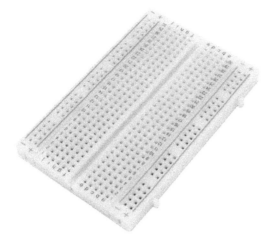

Figure 6.8: Breadboard for quick prototyping

connected with so called breadboards as shown in Figure 6.8. This makes it very fast and cheap to connect own peripherals for a prototypical implementation. The real magic however is the firmware already programmed on the Z-Wave ASIC. It contains all major command classes and functions of Z-Wave. The only task left is to pick the right functions and connect them with the right I/O pins. Simple applications like a binary switch require less than 20 lines of Arduino code. The website zuno.z-wave.me gives a full reference of the functions plus plenty of examples.

Figure 6.9 shows how to build an RGB strip control using ZUNO. The Arduino Code, also available at the web site mentioned, is shown in the listing below. It is only 46 lines of code and readable even for people without extensive knowledge in C or embedded programming.

Listing 6.1: Arduino Scetch for a RGB multicolor light using

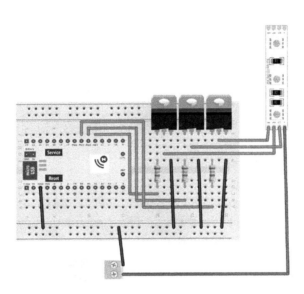

Figure 6.9: RGB Strip control using ZUNO (Source: Z-Wave.Me)

ZUNO

```
#define  REDPIN    PWM1      // pin connection R
#define  GREENPIN  PWM2      // pin connection G
#define  BLUEPIN   PWM3      // pin connection B

ZUNO_SETUP_CHANNELS(
      ZUNO_SWITCH_MULTILEVEL(getRed , setRed),
      ZUNO_SWITCH_MULTILEVEL(getGreen , setGreen),
      ZUNO_SWITCH_MULTILEVEL(getBlue , setBlue));

int  levelRed ;       // will store for R
int  levelGreen ;     // will store for G
int  levelBlue ;      // will store for B

void  setup() {
  pinMode(REDPIN, OUTPUT);
  pinMode(GREENPIN, OUTPUT);
  pinMode(BLUEPIN, OUTPUT);
  Serial.begin();
  Serial.println("start");
  analogWrite(REDPIN,0); // R switch off
  analogWrite(GREENPIN,0); // G switch off
  analogWrite(BLUEPIN,0);} // B switch off

void  loop() { }

int  getRed() { return  levelRed; }
int  getGreen() {return  levelGreen; }
int  getBlue() { return  levelBlue; }

void  setRed(byte value) {
  levelRed = value;
  analogWrite(REDPIN, levelRed*255/99);
  Serial.print("set red = ");
```

```
Serial.println(value);}

void setGreen(byte value) {
  levelGreen = value;
  analogWrite(GREENPIN, levelGreen*255/99);
  Serial.print("set green = ");
  Serial.println(value);}

void setBlue(byte value) {
  levelBlue = value;
  analogWrite(BLUEPIN, levelBlue*255/99);
  Serial.print("set blue = ");
  Serial.println(value);}
```

6.3.4 Z-Way Middleware

The Z-Wave firmware development kit (SDK) or ZUNO allows developing individual devices. The counterpart to this is the controller or IP Gateway. Of course, it is possible to do the same kind of development on the controller side. However Silicon Labs already offers a kind of modem firmware that implements all the controller functions in the firmware of the IC and offers a serial interface protocol to control the IC from a host, e.g. a PC. This serial interface protocol is called Z-Wave Serial Interface Protocol and is used by almost all IP gateways, controllers, or USB sticks with PC software solutions. Some USB sticks like the Z-Wave.Me UZB, shown in Figure 6.10, enhance these basic functions with extensions like frequency switching, backup/restore, or faster data handing. However, the Z-Wave Serial Interface Protocol is the common denominator of all central controller products.

Like the firmware development framework dealing with this protocol has its own pitfalls. There is a countable number of companies in the world that are able to develop a fully functional robust

Figure 6.10: UZB: USB Stick with enhanced functions (Source: Z-Wave.Me)

Z-Wave control stack on top of the `Z-Wave Serial Interface Protocol`. Therefore, certain companies offers the so-called middleware that implements all of the time-critical job handling functions of the Z-Wave protocol layer and allows it to be controlled by a rather simple and fast-to-learn interface on the north bound. Unless there are good reasons to implement a full controller stack from scratch, the use of one of these middleware is strongly suggested. The market offers various options:

- Open Z-Wave: Open Source public domain implementation done as reverse engineering of the protocol, not certified but free of charge.
- ZIPR: A closed source approach with a TCP/IP interface, provided as part of the SDK by Silicon Labs for free.
- Z-Way: A certified well tested commercial solution, among others used in the CIT, RaZberry, etc. It does not only come with the middleware code but as full solution with certified Expert User Interface, etc.

6.3.5 Z-Wave Certification

A Z-Wave device can only be called a Z-Wave device if it is certified by the Z-Wave Alliance. It is not lawful to sell Z-Wave devices and use the Z-Wave brand name to promote devices that are not certified. The certification test process checks if the device conforms to all interoperability requirements. These include:

- Correct definition of the device.
- Implementation of all mandatory Command Classes.
- Correct Implementation of all voluntary Command Classes.
- Correct use of terms and processes in the device manual.
- Minimum radio range requirements.
- Basic quality requirements.

The certification as such is done by independent test houses that publish a test report. All certified devices can be found on the Z-Wave Alliance product data base at products.z-wavealliance.org.

6.4 General information about dimmers

Dimmers are electrical devices. They allow users to continuously dim a light according to the users requirement. There are multiple types of electrical lights, but there is unfortunately no dimmer that can dim all lights.

Lamps can be

- The classical incandescent light invented by Thomas Alva Edison
- Halogen lamps operated by mains power AC (High Voltage Halogen)
- Halogen lamps operated by 24 V (Low Voltage Halogen). The conversion from mains power down to 24 V is done in two different ways: (a) using a simple transformer or (b) using an electronic switching power supply.
- Fluorescent Light in general, and compact fluorescent light (CFL) in particular. They are also called energy saving

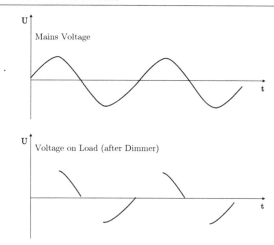

Figure 6.11: Voltage at leading-edge phase control dimmer

lamps.
- Lamps based on Light Emitting Diodes, called LED lights

6.4.1 Leading-edge phase control

Conventional lamps are dimmed using a so-called **leading edge phase control**. This means that a changing portion of the sine wave is cut off. The resulting energy is reduced and the light is dimmed. Figure 6.11 shows a sine wave for full load and for 50% where the sine wave is cut right at 50 %. A special electronic component called TRIAC is used for this function.

At leading edge dimmers, the voltage remains 0V after the wave crossed the zero line. After the defined time, a Triac is ignited. This brings the full voltage of the sine wave to the lamp. The characteristic of a Triac is to block the current again when the sine wave crosses the zero line. Hence, the Triac needs to be ignited at every current wave again.

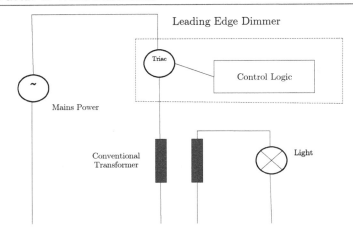

Figure 6.12: Schematics of a leading edge phase control dimmer

Leading edge dimmers work well with incandescent lights and HV halogen light but fail to dim low voltage halogen, fluorescent lamps, and LED lamps. Even worse, they may even destroy these lamps.

6.4.2 Leading Edge Phase Control for inductive loads

Transformers used in low-voltage halogen lamps realize an inductive load. A load is called predominantly inductive if the alternating load current lags behind the alternating voltage of the load. Such a load is also known as lagging load. This means that the voltage is already at zero while the current is not zero yet.

This creates a huge problem for traditional cutting edge dimmers using a Triac. The Triac closes when the current is zero, not when the voltage is zero. This may result in a waveform that does not have symmetric waves for the negative and the positive wave part as shown in Figure 6.13. This, however, results in a DC current

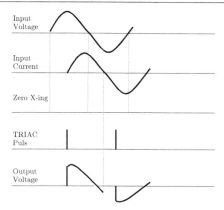

Figure 6.13: Current Shift on inductive loads result in misbalanced waveform

part of the output that may destroy a transformer connected as load.

To dim halogen lamps with conventional transformers, a special electronic is needed to make sure that the Triac switches at the right time. These dimmers can still dim all conventional resistive loads but inductive loads and even slightly reactive loads too.

6.4.3 Trailing Edge Phase Control Dimmer

Electronic power supplies typically represent a conductive load. In a conductive load, the capacitive reactance exceeds the inductive reactance. Hence, the load draws a leading current. To dim these loads, a trailing edge phase control dimmer is needed.

The trailing edge dimmer cuts off the trailing part of the sine wave like shown in Figure 6.14. Such behavior cannot be achieved using a Triac component. High-voltage MOSFET components are used instead. Figure 6.15 shows the schematics of such a dimmer.

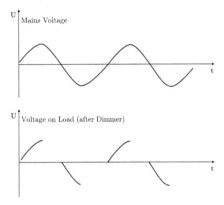

Figure 6.14: Voltage at a trailing edge phase control dimmer

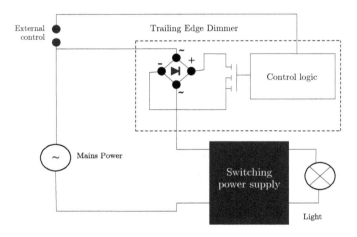

Figure 6.15: Schematics of a trailing edge phase control dimmer

6.4.4   Universal Dimmers

The dilemma of edge phase control dimmers is that (in case of leading edge) either inductive loads or (in case of reactive loads) capacitive loads can be dimmed. The dimmer may even destroy the load not supported.

The solution is a so-called universal dimmer.

Universal dimmers initially detect if the load has inductive or reactive characteristics and change between leading and trailing edge. To make sure the detection delivers the correct result, the user needs to make sure that only one load is connected to the dimmer during power on. Moreover, changing the load later on may result in problems. The biggest challenge of universal dimmers, however, is the higher price point compared to normal leading edge dimmers.

6.4.5   Fluorescent Lamps

Conventional Fluorescent Lights (CFLs) are not dimmable. However, there are special transformer devices capable of dimming these devices. For CFLs, these transformers are already integrated in the lamp socket. CFLs with this unit are called dimmable CFLs and usually have a much higher price.

CFL are typically dimmed either by a trailing edge dimmer or a universal dimmer. Manufacturers of modern CFLs have done a good job in compensating for the reactive load so that even normal leading edge dimmers can dim such a lamp.

6.4.6   LED Lamps

LED lamps can be dimmed very well but neither with leading nor with training edge dimmers. There are dimmers using a so-called PWM (pulse-wide modulation). Hence, LED lights need a special dimmer only applicable for LED lights.

Phases	Leading edge	Leading edge with inductive support	Trailing edge	Universal
Electric light bulb	Yes	Yes	Yes	Yes
HV Halogen	Yes	Yes	Yes	Yes
Low Voltage Halogen (conv. Transformer)	No	Yes	No	Yes
Low Voltage Halogen (Switched power supply)	No	No	Yes	Yes
Dimmable Fluorescent lamp	No	Yes	No	Yes
LED lamp	No	No	No	No

Table 6.1: Conditions to change state for battery operated devices

6.4.7   Dimmer Summary

Table 6.1 gives a summary overview of the different types of dimmers and the types of lamps dimmable.

Appendix A

Useful Online Resources

There are plenty of online resources about Z-Wave. Just Google for Z-Wave or check out YouTube or other media services for content related to Z-Wave. Here are some selected web sites with useful Z-Wave-related content.

http://www.z-wavealliance.org This is the central page for all Z-Wave Alliance members including member section, newsletter management, etc.

http://www.zwaveproducts.com One of the leading online stores for US Z-Wave products

http://www.zwave.com The end user facing page of Z-Wave

http://www.zwave.eu Homepage of the European Master distributor of Z-Wave

http://razberry.z-wave.me The shield board for the famous Raspberry Pi running Z-Way. This software is used in most of the examples of this book.

http://code.google.com/p/open-zwave/   An open source project implementing the Z-Wave protocol

http://manuals.z-wave.info   Central collection of Z-Wave manuals in various languages

http://zwavepublic.com   The complet Application Layer specification of Z-Wave

http://www.vesternet.com   One of the leading online shops dedicated to Z-Wave

https://www.silabs.com/support/z-wave   The most important manufacturer of Z-wave ASICs

Appendix B

Z-Wave Device Types

- Device class Av Control Point
  - Doorbell
  - Specific Device Class Not Used
  - Satellite Receiver
  - Satellite Receiver V2
- Device class Display
  - Specific Device Class Not Used
  - Display (simple) Device Type
- Device class Entry Control
  - Specific Device Class Not Used
  - Door Lock
  - Advanced Door Lock
  - Door Lock (keypad lever) Device Type
  - Door Lock (keypad deadbolt) Device Type
- Device class Generic Controller
  - Specific Device Class Not Used
  - Remote Control Multi Purpose Device Type
  - Portable Scene Controller
  - Portable Installer Tool
  - Remote Control AV Device Type
  - Remote Control Simple Device Type

- Device class Meter
  - Specific Device Class Not Used
  - Sub Energy Meter Device Type
  - Whole Home Energy Meter (Advanced) Device Type
  - Whole Home Meter (Simple) Device Type
- Device class Meter Pulse
  - Specific Device Class Not Used
- Device class Non Interoperable
- Device class Repeater Slave
  - Specific Device Class Not Used
  - Basic Repeater Slave
- Device class Security Panel
  - Zoned Security Panel
- Device class Semi Interoperable
  - Energy Production
  - Specific Device Class Not Used
- Device class Sensor Alarm
  - ADV Zensor Net Alarm Sensor
  - ADV Zensor Net Smoke Sensor
  - Basic Routing Alarm Sensor
  - Basic Routing Smoke Sensor
  - Basic Zensor Net Alarm Sensor
  - Basic Zensor Net Smoke Sensor
  - Specific Device Class Not Used
  - Routing Alarm Sensor
  - Routing Smoke Sensor
  - Zensor Net Alarm Sensor
  - Zensor Net Smoke Sensor
  - Sensor Alarm Device Type
- Device class Sensor Binary
  - Specific Device Class Not Used
  - Routing Binary Sensor
- Device class Sensor Multilevel
  - Specific Device Class Not Used

- Sensor Multilevel Device Type
- Chimney Fan
- Device class Static Controller
  - Specific Device Class Not Used
  - Central Controller Device Type
  - Scene Controller
  - Static Installer Tool
  - Set Top Box Device Type
  - Sub System Controller Device Type
  - TV Device Type
  - Gateway Device Type
- Device class Switch Binary
  - Specific Device Class Not Used
  - On/Off Power Switch Device Type
  - Binary Scene Switch
  - Power Strip Device Type
  - Siren Device Type
  - Valve (open/close) Device Type
- Device class Switch Multilevel
  - Window Covering No Position/Endpoint Device Type
  - Window Covering Endpoint Aware Device Type
  - Window Covering Position/Endpoint Aware Device Type
  - Multiposition Motor
  - Specific Device Class Not Used
  - Light Dimmer Switch Device Type
  - Multilevel Scene Switch
  - Fan Switch Device Type
- Device class Switch Remote
  - Specific Device Class Not Used
  - Binary Remote Switch
  - Multilevel Remote Switch
  - Binary Toggle Remote Switch
  - Multilevel Toggle Remote Switch

- Device class Switch Toggle
  - Specific Device Class Not Used
  - Binary Toggle Switch
  - Multilevel Toggle Switch
- Device class Thermostat
  - Specific Device Class Not Used
  - Setback Schedule Thermostat
  - Thermostat (Setback) Device Type
  - Setpoint Thermostat
  - Thermostat General
  - Thermostat (HVAC) Device Type
  - Thermostat Heating
- Device class Ventilation
  - Specific Device Class Not Used
  - Residential Hrv
- Device class Window Covering
  - Specific Device Class Not Used
  - Simple Window Covering Control
- Device class Zip Gateway
  - Specific Device Class Not Used
  - ZIP Adv Gateway
  - ZIP Tun Gateway
- Device class Zip Node
  - Specific Device Class Not Used
  - ZIP Adv Node
  - ZIP Tun Node
- Device class Wall Controllers
  - Wall Controller Device Type

Appendix C

Z-Wave Command Classes Reference

Hex	Dec	Name
0x20	32	**BASIC**
0x21	33	CONTROLLER REPLICATION
0x22	34	**APPLICATION STATUS**
0x23	35	ZIP
0x24	36	SECURITY PANEL MODE
0x25	37	**SWITCH BINARY**
0x26	38	**SWITCH MULTILEVEL**
0x27	39	**SWITCH ALL**
0x28	40	*SWITCH TOGGLE BINARY*
0x29	41	*SWITCH TOGGLE MULTILEVEL*
0x2A	42	CHIMNEY FAN
0x2B	43	SCENE ACTIVATION
0x2C	44	SCENE ACTUATOR CONF
0x2D	45	SCENE CONTROLLER CONF
0x2E	46	SECURITY PANEL ZONE
0x2F	47	SECURITY PANEL ZONE SENSOR
0x30	48	**SENSOR BINARY**

0x31	49	**SENSOR MULTILEVEL**
0x32	50	**METER**
0x33	51	**COLOR CONTROL**
0x34	52	NETWORK MANAGEMENT IN-CLUSION
0x35	53	*METER PULSE*
0x36	54	BASIC TARIFF INFO
0x37	55	HRV STATUS
0x38	56	THERMOSTAT HEATING
0x39	57	HRV CONTROL
0x3A	58	DCP CONFIG
0x3B	59	DCP MONITOR
0x3C	60	METER TBL CONFIG
0x3D	61	METER TBL MONITOR
0x3E	62	METER TBL PUSH
0x3F	63	PREPAYMENT
0x40	64	THERMOSTAT MODE
0x41	65	PREPAYMENT ENCAPSULATION
0x42	66	**THERMOSTAT OPERATING STATE**
0x43	67	**THERMOSTAT SETPOINT**
0x44	68	**THERMOSTAT FAN MODE**
0x45	69	**THERMOSTAT FAN STATE**
0x46	70	CLIMATE CONTROL SCHEDULE
0x47	71	**THERMOSTAT SETBACK**
0x48	72	RATE TBL CONFIG
0x49	73	RATE TBL MONITOR
0x4A	74	TARIFF CONFIG
0x4B	75	TARIFF TBL MONITOR
0x4C	76	**DOOR LOCK LOGGING**
0x4D	77	NETWORK MANAGEMENT BASIC
0x4E	78	*SCHEDULE ENTRY LOCK*
0x4F	79	ZIP 6LOWPAN

0x50	80	*BASIC WINDOW COVERING*
0x51	81	*MTP WINDOW COVERING*
0x52	82	NETWORK MANAGEMENT PROXY
0x53	83	SCHEDULE
0x54	84	NETWORK MANAGEMENT PRIMARY
0x55	85	TRANSPORT SERVICE
0x56	86	CRC 16 ENCAP
0x57	87	APPLICATION CAPABILITY
0x58	88	ZIP ND
0x59	89	**ASSOCIATION GRP INFO**
0x5A	90	**DEVICE RESET LOCALLY**
0x5B	91	**CENTRAL SCENE**
0x5C	92	IP ASSOCIATION
0x5D	93	ANTITHEFT
0x5E	94	**ZWAVEPLUS INFO**
0x5F	95	ZIP GATEWAY
0x60	96	**MULTI CHANNEL**
0x61	97	ZIP PORTAL
0x62	98	**DOOR LOCK**
0x63	99	**USER CODE**
0x64	100	
0x65	101	DMX
0x66	102	BARRIER OPERATOR
0x67	103	NETWORK MANAGEMENT INSTALL
0x68	104	ZIP NAMING
0x69	105	MAILBOX
0x6A	106	WINDOW COVERING
0x6B	107	IRRIGATION
0x6C	108	**SUPERVISION**
0x6D	109	

0x6E	110	
0x6F	111	
0x70	112	**CONFIGURATION**
0x71	113	**ALARM now NOTIFICATION**
0x72	114	**MANUFACTURER SPECIFIC**
0x73	115	**POWERLEVEL**
0x74	116	
0x75	117	**PROTECTION**
0x76	118	LOCK
0x77	119	NODE NAMING
0x78	120	
0x79	121	
0x7A	122	**FIRMWARE UPDATE MD**
0x7B	123	*GROUPING NAME*
0x7C	124	*REMOTE ASSOCIATION ACTIVATE*
0x7D	125	*REMOTE ASSOCIATION*
0x7E	126	
0x7F	127	
0x80	128	**BATTERY**
0x81	129	**CLOCK**
0x82	130	*HAIL*
0x83	131	
0x84	132	**WAKE UP**
0x85	133	**ASSOCIATION**
0x86	134	**VERSION**
0x87	135	**INDICATOR**
0x88	136	*PROPRIETARY*
0x89	137	LANGUAGE
0x8A	138	**TIME**
0x8B	139	TIME PARAMETERS
0x8C	140	GEOGRAPHIC LOCATION

0x8D	141	
0x8E	142	**MULTI CHANNEL ASSOCIATION**
0x8F	143	**MULTI CMD**
0x90	144	ENERGY PRODUCTION
0x91	145	MANUFACTURER PROPRIETARY
0x92	146	SCREEN MD
0x93	147	SCREEN ATTRIBUTES
0x94	148	SIMPLE AV CONTROL
0x95	149	AV CONTENT DIRECTORY MD
0x96	150	AV RENDERER STATUS
0x97	151	AV CONTENT SEARCH MD
0x98	152	**SECURITY V1**
0x99	153	AV TAGGING MD
0x9A	154	IP CONFIGURATION
0x9B	155	ASSOCIATION COMMAND CONFIG
0x9C	156	**SENSOR ALARM**
0x9D	157	SILENCE ALARM
0x9E	158	**SENSOR CONFIGURATION**
0x9F	159	**SECURITY S2**

Table C.1: SDK 6.71 (Feb. 2017, *deprecated*, **important**)

Appendix D

Frequencies by Country

Region	Standard	Z-Wave Frequency
Algeria	ETSI EN 300 220	868.40 MHz, 869.85 MHz
Argentina	FCC CFR47 Part 15.249	908.40 MHz, 916.00 MHz
Armenia	ETSI EN 300 220	868.40 MHz, 869.85 MHz
Australia	AS/NZS 4268	919.80 MHz, 921.40 MHz
Bahamas	FCC CFR47 Part 15.249	908.40 MHz, 916.00 MHz
Bahrain	ETSI EN 300 220	868.40 MHz, 869.85 MHz
Barbados	FCC CFR47 Part 15.249	908.40 MHz, 916.00 MHz
Bermuda	FCC CFR47 Part 15.249	908.40 MHz, 916.00 MHz
Bolivia	FCC CFR47 Part 15.249	908.40 MHz, 916.00 MHz

Brazil	ANATEL Resolution 506	919.80 MHz, 921.40 MHz
British Virgin Islands	FCC CFR47 Part 15.249	908.40 MHz, 916.00 MHz
Canada	FCC CFR47 Part 15.249	908.40 MHz, 916.00 MHz
Cayman Islands	FCC CFR47 Part 15.249	908.40 MHz, 916.00 MHz
CEPT	EN 300 220	868.40 MHz, 869.85 MHz
Chile	FCC CFR47 Part 15.249	919.80 MHz, 921.40 MHz, 921.42 MHz
China	CNAS/EN 300 220	868.40 MHz
Colombia	FCC CFR47 Part 15.249	908.40 MHz, 916.00 MHz
Costa Rica	ARIB T96, ARIB STD-T108	922.50 MHz, 923.09 MHz, 926.30 MHz
Ecuador	FCC CFR47 Part 15.249	908.40 MHz, 916.00 MHz
Egypt	ETSI EN 300 220	868.40 MHz, 869.85 MHz
El Salvador	AS/NZS 4268	919.80 MHz, 921.40 MHz
EU	EN 300 220	868.40 MHz, 869.85 MHz
French Dept. of Guiana	ETSI EN 300 220	868.40 MHz, 869.85 MHz
Guatemala	FCC CFR47 Part 15.249	908.40 MHz, 916.00 MHz
Haiti	FCC CFR47 Part 15.249	908.40 MHz, 916.00 MHz
Honduras	FCC CFR47 Part 15.249	908.40 MHz, 916.00 MHz

Hong Kong (China)	HKTA 1035	919.80 MHz
India	CSR 564 (E)	865.20 MHz
Indonesia	ETSI EN 300 200	868.40 MHz, 869.85 MHz
Israel		916.00 MHz
Jamaica	FCC CFR47 Part 15.249	908.40 MHz, 916.00 MHz
Japan	ARIB STD-T108	922.50 MHz, 923.90 MHz, 926.30 MHz
Jordan	ETSI EN 300 220	868.40 MHz, 869.85 MHz
Kazakhstan	ETSI EN 300 220	868.40 MHz, 869.85 MHz
Lebanon	ETSI EN 300 220	868.40 MHz, 869.85 MHz
Libya	ETSI EN 300 220	868.40 MHz, 869.85 MHz
Malaysia	MCMC MTSFB TC T007:2014	919.80 MHz, 921.40 MHz, 921.42 MHz
Mauritius	ETSI EN 300 220	868.40 MHz, 869.85 MHz
Mexico	FCC CFR47 Part 15.249	908.40 MHz, 916.00 MHz
New Zealand	AS/NZS 4268	921.40 MHz, 919.80 MHz
Nicaragua	FCC CFR47 Part 15.249	908.40 MHz, 916.00 MHz
Nigeria	ETSI EN 300 220	868.40 MHz, 869.85 MHz
Oman	ETSI EN 300 220	868.40 MHz, 869.85 MHz

Panama	FCC CFR47 Part 15.249	908.40 MHz, 916.00 MHz
Paraguay	AS/NZS 4268	919.80 MHz, 921.04 MHz
Peru	AS/NZS 4268	919.80 MHz, 921.40 MHz
Qatar	ETSI EN 300 220	868.40 MHz, 869.85 MHz
Russian Federation	GKRCh/ETSI 300 220	869.00 MHz
Saudi Arabia	ETSI EN 300 220	868.40 MHz, 869.85 MHz
Singapore	TS SRD/ETSI 300 220	868.40 MHz, 869.85 MHz
South Africa	ICASA/ETSI 300 220	868.40 MHz, 869.00 MHz
Republic of Korea	Clause 2, Article 58-2 of Radio Waves Act	920.90 MHz, 921.70 MHz, 923.10 MHz
St Kitts and Nevis	FCC CFR47 Part 15.249	908.40 MHz, 916.00 MHz
Suriname	FCC CFR47 Part 15.249	908.40 MHz, 916.00 MHz
Taiwan (China)	NCC/LP0002	922.50 MHz, 923.90 MHz, 926.30 MHz
Trinidad and Tabago	FCC CFR47 Part 15.249	908.40 MHz, 916.00 MHz
Turks and Caicos Islands	FCC CFR47 Part 15.249	908.40 MHz, 916.00 MHz
UAE	ETSI EN 300 220	868.40 MHz, 869.85 MHz
Uruguay	AS/NZS 4268	919.80 MHz, 921.40 MHz

USA	FCC CFR47 Part 15.249	908.40 MHz, 916.00 MHz
Yemen	ETSI EN 300 220	868.40 MHz, 869.85 MHz

Table D.1: Frequencies by Country

Bibliography

[Mitsumi2011] Mitsumi Electric Co, Ltd Press Release :*Mitsumi concluded Z-Wave Module Supply Agreement with Sigma Designs, Inc. in USA* , May23rd, 2011, http://www.mitsumi.co.jp/pdf/20110523_e.pdf

[ITU2012] ITU-T G.9959: *Short range narrowband digital radiocommunication transceivers - PHY & MAC layer specification*, International Telecommunication Union, 02/2012

[Merten2008] Merten CONNECT Produkt Literatur, *www.merten.com*

[SmartHome2017] *http://de.wikipedia.org/wiki/Smart_Home*

[6LoWPAN2017] *http://de.wikipedia.org/wiki/6LoWPAN*

[Merten2007] Homepage: *http://www.merten.com*

[CEPT2017] *http://de.wikipedia.org/wiki/CEPT*

[Tutorial2015] *http://www.electronics-tutorials.ws/boolean/bool_6.html*

[Givant2008] Givant, Steven, Halmos, Paul: *Introduction to Boolean Algebras*, Springer-Verlag New York, 978-0-387-68436-9

[Zme2017] Homepage: *www.zwave.me*

[Sigma2008] Press Release Sigma Designs Dec, 18th, 2008: *Sigma Designs Acquires Zensys* http://www.silicontap.com/sigma_designs_acquires-_zensys/s-0019088.html

[Fouladi2013] Bahrang Fouladi, Shand Ghanoun: *Honey, I am Home!!, Hacking Z-Wave Home Automation Systems*, Black Hat USA 2013, Las Vegas July 27-Aug1st, 2013, Slides available at http://www.slideshare.net/sensepost/hacking-zwave-home-automation-systems

[Hall2016] Joseph Hall and Ben Ramsey: *Z-WAVE PROTOCOL HACKED WITH SDR*, Hackaday 16. January 2016, Story available at http://hackaday.com/2016/01/16/shmoocon-2016-z-wave-protocol-hacked-with-sdr/

[Markoffnov2016] John Markoffnov: *Why Light Bulbs May Be the Next Hacker Target* New York Times, Nov 3rd, 2016, https://www.nytimes.com/2016/11/03/technology-/why-light-bulbs-may-be-the-next-hacker-target.html

[Sigma2017] *Z-Wave Alliance Announces New Security Requirements for All Z-Wave Certified IoT Devices*, Press Release Z-Wave Alliance, Nov. 17th, 2016, http://z-wavealliance.org/z-wave-alliance-announces-new-security-requirements-z-wave-certified-iot-devices/

[Alliance2012] *Z-Wave Alliance Announces 700th Certified Product*, Press Release Z-Wave Alliance, Sept. 4th, 2012, http://z-wavealliance.org/z-wave-alliance-announces-700th-certified-product/

[Alliance2014] *Z-Wave Extends Smart Home Market Leadership With 1000th Certified Product*, Press Release Z-Wave Alliance, May 2014, http://z-wavealliance.org/z-wave-extends-smart-home-market-leadership-1000th-certified-product/

[Sigma2016] Z-Wave Public Application Layer Specification, www.zwavepublic.com

[Alliance2017] Z-Wave Alliance: Certified Installer Tookit

[Edhc2013] *Elliptic Curve Diffie-Hellman cryptography*, http://nvlpubs.nist.gov/nistpubs/SpecialPublications/ NIST.SP.800-56Ar2.pdf

[Bernstein2006] D. J. Bernstein: *Curve25519: new Diffie-Hellman speed records* Proceedings of PKC 2006. URL: http://cr.yp.to/papers.html

[Aes2001] - *FIPS197: Advanced Encryption Standard (AES)*, November 26, 2001, URL: http://csrc.nist.gov/publications/fips/fips197/fips-197.pdf

[Paetz2013] Paetz, Christian; Volkmar, Andre: *Das 868 MHz Frequenzband zwischen Kurzstreckenfunk und LTE*, elektronik wireless, October 2013, pp34-38

[Nsa2003] *National Policy on the Use of the Advanced Encryption Standard (AES) to Protect National Security Systems and National Security Information*, June 2003, http://csrc.nist.gov/groups/ST/toolkit/documents/aes/ CNSS15FS.pdf

[Diffie1976] - Diffie, W.; Hellman, M. (1976). *New directions in cryptography* IEEE Transactions on Information Theory 22 (6): 644654. Introduction to DH: https://www.khanacademy.org-/computing/computer-science/cryptography-/modern-crypt/v/diffiehellman- key-exchange-part-1 https://www.khanacademy.org/computing/computer-science/ cryptography/ modern-crypt/v/diffie-hellman-key-exchange-part-2

[Sigma2011] *Sigma Designs, SDS13349, Security considerations in Home Control installations*

[Sigma2017] *Sigma Designs, SDS11274, Security 2 Command Class, version 1*

[Sigma2013] *Sigma Designs, ZM5101 General Purpose Z-Wave SiP Module*

List of Tables

1.1   Summary of Pros and Cons of different radio tech-
      nologies   31

2.1   Structure of the frequency band   45
2.2   Saw Filter and Frequency Restrictions   49
2.3   Attenuation of different material [Merten2008]   . .   58
2.4   Work Sheet to determine the wireless distance . . .   59

3.1   Z-Wave Channels   68
3.2   Transmission times of minimal and maximal PHY
      frames   72
3.3   Home-ID and Node-ID   76
3.4   Bit Assignment of MAC Frame   80
3.5   Properties of the Z-Wave device models   97
3.6   Typical applications for slaves   98
3.7   Possible combinations of node types 107
3.8   Comparison of different Z-Wave network manage-
      ment modes   124
3.9   Different valid network configurations 129

4.1   Conditions to change state for battery-operated
      devices 154
4.2   Power consumptions of different chip generation . . 155

4.3   Battery lifetime if no static controller is present
       (for Series 500 ICs) 156
4.4   Battery lifetime with active static controller (for
       Series 500 ICs, 1000 mAh battery) 157
4.5   Comparison of scenes and associations 180

5.1   Troubleshooting on Z-Wave networks 250
5.2   Comparison betwen CIT and Expert UI 251

6.1   Conditions to change state for battery operated
       devices 281

C.1   SDK 6.71 (Feb. 2017, *deprecated*, **important**) . . 292

D.1   Frequencies by Country 297

List of Figures

1.1   Traditional home of the late 1990s 13
1.2   First step into Smart Home 14
1.3   Second step into Smart Home 15
1.4   Final step into Smart Home 16
1.5   Generic four layers of a wireless communication
      network 20
1.6   Z-Wave Controller made by Zensys in 2001 32
1.7   Z-Wave Alliance Website (as of 2017) 33
1.8   ASIC Series 500 35
1.9   Evolution from proprietary solution to public stan-
      dard 36
1.10 Z-Wave Plus Logo 38
1.11 Z-Wave Logo evolution 39

2.1   Attenuation of radio signals by a wall 41
2.2   Model's transmission path between sender and re-
      ceiver 42
2.3   ITU Region Split of the World 43
2.4   Members of the CEPT-Organization in Europe . . 44
2.5   FCC Logo 47
2.6   Z-Way User Interface for Frequency Switching . . . 48
2.7   ZM5202 Module with Filter identifier 50
2.8   Background Noise 53

2.9 Comparison of two Antenna Designs 54

2.10 Performance of a Helix antenna 55

2.11 Dedicated Z-Wave Antenna on an industrial Z-Wave Gateway 56

2.12 Dedicated wire as Z-Wave antenna 57

2.13 PCBA Antenna 57

2.14 Effective wall thickness 59

2.15 Radio shadow by metallic structures 60

2.16 Signal gain by constructive or in-phase interference 61

2.17 Signal attenuation by destructive or out-of-phase interference 62

2.18 Fading of Link between nodes 63

2.19 Wireless Range versus Link Margin 64

2.20 Transmitting power of Z-Wave compared to cell phone 65

3.1 Frequency Spectrum 69

3.2 Manchester-Encoding 70

3.3 NRZ-Encoding 71

3.4 Z-Wave (PHY/MAC) Wireless Frame 72

3.5 Z-Wave devices before inclusion in a network . . . 77

3.6 Network after successful Inclusion 78

3.7 Two Z-Wave-Networks with different Home-IDs coexist 78

3.8 Transport Frame Layout for Singlecast 80

3.9 Transport Frame Layout for Multicast 81

3.10 Communication with and without acknowledgement 85

3.11 Network without routing 86

3.12 Z-Wave network with routing 87

3.13 Maximum route between 2 nodes via 4 repeaters . 88

3.14 Routing Table 89

3.15 Example of a meshed network 90

3.16 Routing Table for Example network 90

3.17 Routing from Node 1 via Node 3 to Node 6 91

3.18 Multiple communication attempts in Z-Wave - step 1 91

3.19 Multiple communication attempts in Z-Wave - step 2 92

3.20 Multiple communication attempts in Z-Wave - step 3 93

3.21 Routing Information changes the Transport Frame 94

3.22 CO2 sensor 99

3.23 Z-Weather 101

3.24 Remote Control with manual wakeup 104

3.25 Sensor with wakeup interval 105

3.26 Wakeup-Beam wakes up a FLiRS device 106

3.27 Siren as FLiRS device 107

3.28 Z-Wave Controller with a button to exclude a failed node 111

3.29 Z-Wave Controller that allows to mark nodes as failed 112

3.30 Webbrowser Interface for Network Reorganisation . 114

3.31 SUC in a Z-Wave-Network 117

3.32 Update of the Routing table in a SUC 117

3.33 SIS Server in a Z-Wave network 119

3.34 Explorer frame Layout 120

3.35 Explorer frame in Action 121

3.36 Z-Wave Network with one portable controller . . . 125

3.37 Example of a network with one static controller . . 126

3.38 Z-Wave network with a static and a portable controller 127

3.39 Z-Wave Network with SUC 129

4.1 Z-Wave Controllers, Sensors and Actors 132

4.2 Examples of different command classes 136

4.3 Frame Layout for Command Classes 137

4.4   **Basic** Command Class 139

4.5   Optionally, recommended and mandatory Command Classes within a device class 140

4.6   Different Implementation of a Device Class Binary Power Switch by different vendors 141

4.7   Fibaro Wall Plug 142

4.8   Node Information Frame 146

4.9   Device Interview 147

4.10   Generic configuration in PC Software 149

4.11   User-friendly configuration in PC Software 150

4.12   Sleeping and wakeup 152

4.13   Wakeup time dialog 153

4.14   AAA Battery 153

4.15   Multichannel Command Class Encapsulation . . . 159

4.16   How a trigger works 162

4.17   All nodes in an association group receive a signal when the event happens. 163

4.18   Scene execution 168

4.19   In-Wall Scene Controller, manufactured by Cooper 169

4.20   Scene setting in Z-Way 171

4.21   User Interface defining timers and schedules 173

4.22   User Interface defining Boolean rules and logic . . 178

4.23   Dedicated buttons on a remote control 182

4.24   Setup for Associations 183

4.25   Example of a smart home user interface on a mobile device 184

4.26   Secure communication using nonces 188

4.27   Encryption using AES128 191

4.28   Security Command Class V1 Encapsulation 192

4.29   Z-Wave S2: QR code example 196

4.30   Diffi-Hellman Key Exchange 197

4.31 Z-Wave Classic: Authentication by push a button
     on the device 200
4.32 Request of different network keys 201
4.33 Z-Wave S2: Authenticated Access 202
4.34 Request for pin code 203
4.35 Z-Wave S2 List of devices 203

5.1 North American smart wall switch 210
5.2 Schematics of Wall Insert installation 211
5.3 Wall Insert behind wall switch 211
5.4 Wall controller with special button 216
5.5 Inclusion function in central controller 217
5.6 Smart Start: Scanning QR code 218
5.7 Smart Start: Checking Inclusion Request 219
5.8 Smart Start: User Interface for DSK (Device Key) 220
5.9 Controller-Replication 222
5.10 Primary Change Function in PC software 223
5.11 User Interface to allow individual polling 230
5.12 Expert User Interface of Z-Way 233
5.13 CIT device 234
5.14 Background Noise 235
5.15 Realtime Measurement of Background-Noise 236
5.16 Powerbank to power the CIT for mobile use 237
5.17 Network Statistics Display 238
5.18 Status Page Expert User Interface / CIT 239
5.19 Packet Sniffer 240
5.20 Paket timing of a fresh Z-Wave network 241
5.21 Paket timing of an aged Z-Wave network 242
5.22 Neighbor-Table of a controller 244
5.23 Link test of a node 245
5.24 Poltorak-Chart 246
5.25 Association Dialog 248

5.26 1st generation Z-Wave product, made by Advanced Control Technologies 253

6.1 Different layers of Z-Wave and its legal status . . . 258
6.2 ITU-T G.9959 259
6.3 SDK Version shown in Z-Way Software 264
6.4 Z-Wave ASIC Building blocks 265
6.5 Schematics of a single button controller 266
6.6 Z-Wave System Development Kit Hardware 268
6.7 ZUNO 269
6.8 Breadboard for quick prototyping 270
6.9 RGB Strip control using ZUNO 271
6.10 UZB 274
6.11 Voltage at leading-edge phase control dimmer . . . 276
6.12 Schematics of a leading edge phase control dimmer 277
6.13 Current Shift on inductive loads result in misbalanced waveform 278
6.14 Voltage at a trailing edge phase control dimmer . . 279
6.15 Schematics of a trailing edge phase control dimmer 279

www.ingramcontent.com/pod-product-compliance
Lightning Source LLC
Chambersburg PA
CBHW071104050326
40690CB00008B/1114